Accession no.
36095637

D023997

Art through Music

Claire Tinker

LIS - LIBRARY	
Date 21.01.10	Fund e
Order No. 2070844	
University of Chester	

Acknowledgements

The author and publisher would like to thank the children from Hunters Bar and Nook Lane Junior Schools for, once again, demonstrating their amazing enthusiasm and artistic talents. The author would particularly like to thank all the staff at these two schools and the head teachers Jill Hallsworth and Gina Hodges for being truly wonderful believers in the creative arts and supporting the work so generously. A big thank you to all family and friends, especially Theo Spyrou, for their encouragement and creative inspirational contributions to this book.

The publisher would also like to thank Caz Gillies for her help with the musical references.

Mardi Gras Carnival Masks (page 10)

© 2007 Belair Publications on behalf of the author.

Apex Business Centre, Boscombe Road, Dunstable, LU5 4RL
Email: belair@folens.com

Belair Publications are protected by international copyright laws. All rights reserved.

The copyright of all materials in this publication, except where otherwise stated, remains the property of the publisher and author. No part of this publication may be reproduced, stored in a retrieval system, or transmitted, in any form or by any means, for whatever purpose, without the written permission of Belair Publications.

Claire Tinker hereby asserts her moral right to be identified as the author of this work in accordance with the Copyright, Designs and Patents Act 1988.

Commissioning Editor: Zoë Nichols   Editor: Melody Ismail
Page Layout: Barbara Linton   Photography: Roger Brown
Cover Design: Steve West

First published in 2007 by Belair Publications.

Every effort has been made to trace the copyright holders of material used in this publication.
If any copyright holder has been overlooked, we should be pleased to make the necessary arrangements.

British Library Cataloguing in Publication Data. A catalogue record for this publication is available from the British Library.

ISBN 978 1 84191 458 9

Contents

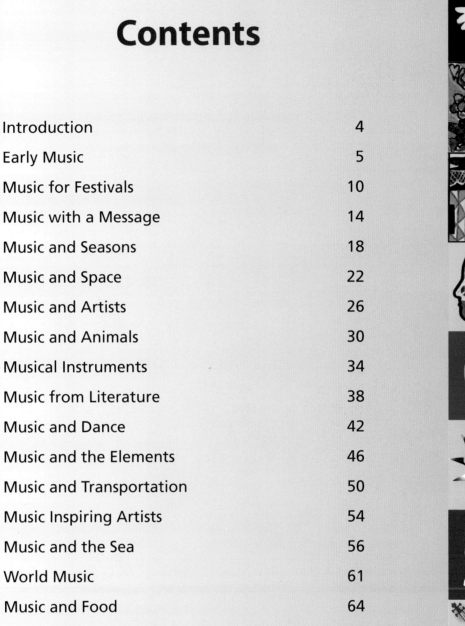

Introduction

Music, as with the visual arts, has the power to deeply affect our state of mind, stir our emotions and evoke a response. Music and art have always been intrinsically linked with many artists being profoundly inspired by music and numerous musicians composing in response to visual stimuli. The aim of this book is to explore this special relationship and find ways in which music can be integrated into art practice. It is not hard to find examples of the marriage of these two creative disciplines, not least in theatre work, musicals, ballets and festivals.

The projects in this book demonstrate how music can be employed to inspire a visual response. Each of the 17 chapters is linked to a particular theme or genre of music and most have a short musical activity other than pure listening as a starting point. The emphasis however has been on the visual arts and display using a familiar piece of music as inspiration. The musical activities are therefore brief and merely intended to support the appreciation, enjoyment and delivery of the music curriculum. The collection of music used in this book is wide-ranging, from nursery rhymes to classical music, many examples may already be in schools' CD libraries. As always, the Internet is an invaluable source for researching and reading lyrics, and tracking down publishers and suppliers of unfamiliar musical works. There are literally thousands of websites with music to listen to and use of the internet will enable children to listen to most of the types of music described in this book.

The activities employ many different materials and techniques to produce two- and three-dimensional artwork with clear step-by-step instructions and further cross-curricular links to investigate. I am convinced you do not have to be an expert to explore the enjoyment of music in the classroom; in fact the musical activities in this book do not presuppose any particular expertise either on the part of the teacher or the children. It simply aims to present and perhaps demystify some genres of music to enable teachers to encourage their children to listen, enjoy and be inspired enough to dance, sing and above all be creative in the visual arts.

Claire Tinker

Matisse Display (page 55)

Medieval Manuscripts

The term 'early music' is generally used to describe Western music that was composed before 1750. In Europe during the Middle Ages (around 500 to 1500), music was an important part of worship in the Christian Church. Church services were sung rather than spoken and medieval monks chanted their prayers, all singing the same tune with no harmonies. This was called 'plainsong'. Over time, music became more complicated and the need to record it became apparent; in the 11th century a monk called Guido d'Arezzo developed a way of notating music using a set of lines called a staff or stave to show the pitch of notes. Medieval manuscripts of religious music show musical notes as black diamonds and rectangles written on four red lines. These staves were beautifully copied by hand and richly decorated by monks.

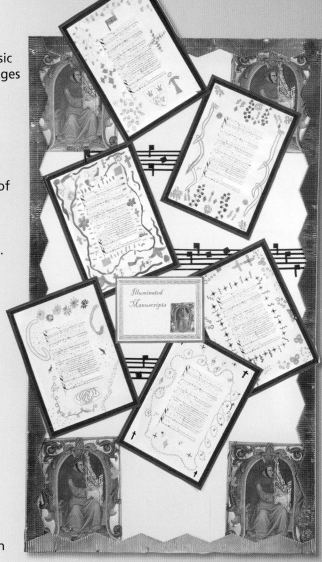

Resources

- Medieval music
- Examples of medieval scores and manuscripts
- Copies of musical scores
- Tea bags and water
- Ink pens and coloured ink

Approach

1. Listen to some early medieval music, such as, *Medieval English Music* (Musique D'abord, 1997). Explain to the children that printing was invented in the West by a German named Johannes Gutenberg in the middle of the 15th century and before this, music had to be copied out by hand. Explain how the monks produced magnificent and beautifully decorated manuscripts by hand. Show the children examples.

2. Ask the children to imagine that they are monks who have to decorate a musical manuscript. If possible, give them a photocopy of an early score (without decoration), or they could draw their own with black diamonds and rectangles on red, four-line staves.

3. Stain the manuscripts using wet tea bags to give an old, distressed appearance.

4. When dry, use ink pens and coloured ink to richly decorate the manuscript. To create a monastic atmosphere, dim the lights and play some medieval church music in the background – insist on silence!

5. Display the children's work with reproductions of medieval manuscripts.

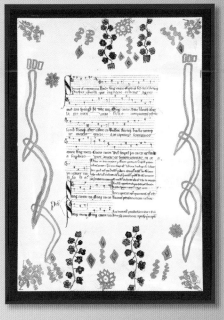

Cross-curricular Links

HISTORY: Study the implications and importance of Gutenberg's invention of printing. Discuss how it changed the production of music and literature.

Tudor Portraits

Resources

- Copies of portraits by Hans Holbein
- Tudor music
- Viewfinders
- Small sheets of canvas or card
- Acrylic paints and brushes

Approach

1. Explain to the children that much of what we know about early musical instruments comes from pictorial evidence and the best-known paintings were commissioned by rich, powerful people. One of the most famous Tudor portrait painters was Hans Holbein (1497–1543), a German artist who was asked by Henry VIII to paint members of the royal household. Discuss the contents of one of his paintings, such as *The Ambassadors* (1533). The picture is full of hidden references and interesting objects. Find the musical instrument and research what it could be.

2. Listen to some Tudor music, such as *Pastime With Good Company* by Henry VIII from *English Madrigals and Songs* (Naxos, 1999).

3. Display a copy of *Henry VIII* by Hans Holbein (1536) and help the children engage with the picture by asking them questions: What can you tell about Henry from the portrait? Why do you think he wanted his portrait painted? What sort of image is he trying to portray? What does his facial expression tell us about his character? Henry VIII was an accomplished musician; use the Internet to find out more about his musical skills and the instruments he would have played.

4. Provide the children with a viewfinder and ask them to highlight a part of the Holbein painting which most interests them – such as a close up of Henry's head and shoulders.

5. Discuss what sort of medium has been used in the original painting and how it has been applied. Look at the colours that have been used.

6. Give the children a small piece of canvas and thick acrylic paints.

7. Ask the children to use a sharp pencil to sketch the main outline of their highlighted area onto the canvas. Mix paint as thickly as possible and apply using a variety of thicknesses of brushes.

Cross-curricular Links

HISTORY: Research the origins and spread of the plague that killed Holbein in 1543.

PE: Introduce the children to Tudor and Elizabethan dances.

Renaissance Stained Glass Windows

The term 'Renaissance', meaning 'rebirth', is used to describe the period from roughly 1450 to 1600. The new ideas about architecture, literature, art and music began in Italy in the 14th century and were inspired by Ancient Greek culture. During the Renaissance, composers often wrote their best music for the church. The most popular instruments were the lute, harp and a type of organ called a portative organ. In the larger churches there might have been music especially written for Christmas, in addition to the chanting and choral music of ordinary services. Churches and chapels were decorated with stained glass windows, which mixed Italian Renaissance designs with English ideas.

Resources

- Renaissance music
- Pictures of stained glass windows
- Large sheets of acetate
- Glass paints and outliners
- Paper and felt pens

Approach

1. Listen to some Renaissance church music such as *The Best of the Renaissance* (Tallis Scholars, 1999). Explain that people often played and sang in small groups called 'consorts'. The lute was a popular Renaissance instrument.

2. Show the children examples of stained glass windows and explain how they were made by the artist. Drawing the design on a table, the artist marked the sizes, positions and colours of the shapes. A hot iron tool was used to cut out the shapes which were painted and then heated in a kiln to solder the pieces together. Lead was moulded round each piece and they were then joined together like a jigsaw puzzle.

3. Give the children a square of paper and ask them to design a stained glass window, using the examples as inspiration.

4. Place the designs (in no particular order) on a table. Cover with a sheet of acetate and trace over the outline of each individual design.

5. The children could use outliners and glass paints to complete their windows.

6. Display against a window to show the transparent painting effect to the best advantage.

Cross-curricular Links

ICT: Leonardo da Vinci (1452–1519) is considered one of the greatest minds of all time. He is a celebrated scientist, engineer, inventor and artist. The children could use the Internet to research the life and work of this talented Renaissance man.

Baroque Violins

The term 'Baroque' describes the characteristics of artistic expression from around 1600 to 1750. It means 'elaborately and richly decorated' and was a word originally used to describe the twisting, curling patterns of architecture of the 17th century. To some people of the time, the music seemed to be full of decorative twists and turns, and Baroque describes the music of this period containing elaborate ornamentation and contrasting elements. The most famous composers of Baroque music are Johann Sebastian Bach (1685–1750), George Frideric Handel (1685–1759) and Antonio Vivaldi (1678–1741). The two most popular instruments were violin and harpsichord. During this time, the makers of these two instruments were some of the finest there have ever been and included Antonio Stradivari (1644–1737). Baroque violins were sometimes very elaborately decorated with carved backs.

Resources

- Baroque music
- Pictures of Baroque art and architecture
- Viewfinders
- Card templates of violins
- Pencils, string, glue and scissors
- Paint and brushes

Approach

1. Explain the term 'Baroque' and put this genre in a historical context using a timeline. Listen to some Baroque music, such as, *Concerto in D Minor for Two Violins* by Bach, *The Four Seasons* by Vivaldi and *Water Music* by Handel.

2. Encourage the children to identify the instruments; (mainly violin and harpsichord, but there are also cello, double bass, viola and oboe, horn, trumpet and drums in the *Water Music*).

3. Show the children pictures of Baroque art and architecture. Use ICT to collect examples. Reiterate that Baroque means 'richly decorated'. Children could use viewfinders to highlight areas of design they find particularly interesting.

4. Give the children a card template of a violin and ask them to sketch an interesting Baroque pattern in pencil on the template.

5. Cover the design with string, allow glue to dry, and paint.

Cross-curricular Links

HISTORY: Baroque composers were employed by the nobility or the church and they were expected to write music to order for religious services or for entertainment. This system was called patronage. George I of England (crowned 1714) was Handel's patron. Study the reign of George I and ask the children to write about his life.

Nativity Scene

George Frideric Handel was a great organist and harpsichordist and he became famous as a composer of operas. He successfully followed the changing musical fashions and in the 1730s, when concert audiences grew tired of opera, he began to write oratorios instead. Oratorios are like operas, but have a religious theme and tell stories from the Bible. In an oratorio there is no scenery, costumes or acting. Probably the most famous of all oratorios is *Messiah* by Handel which tells the story of the birth and death of Christ.

Approach

1. Explain to the children the religious connection to oratorios. Play extracts of *Messiah* by Handel. Read the Bible story of the nativity and discuss the musical interpretation of Handel's oratorio.

2. Oratorios were set to orchestral music. Singers took the role of characters; they were accompanied by a chorus and an obvious place to perform them, both then and now, is in a church. Give the children pictures of stained glass windows and explain they are to design one for the nativity story.

3. Give each child a long sheet of paper cut into a window shape. Ask the children to choose one of the people from the nativity story, making sure at least one child has chosen either Mary, Jesus or Joseph. While they work, play extracts from *The Christmas Oratorio* by Bach.

4. Encourage the children to draw, filling their window so that each part of the nativity scene is to the same scale.

5. Once the drawings are complete, children can paint and decorate with sequins.

6. Back a display board with black paper and cut out a large star and ornate patterns in gold. Display in the form of a large stained glass window.

7. Listen to more contemporary music about the birth of Christ, such as carols.

Resources

- *Messiah* by Handel
- *The Christmas Oratorio* by JS Bach
- CD of carols/nativity story
- Pictures of stained glass windows
- Long sheets of paper/card
- Paint and brushes
- Black paper
- Gold paper, sequins and glue

Cross-curricular Links

RE: Look at creation stories. Listen to Joseph Haydn's oratorio *The Creation* (1796) (a Christian creation story).

Carnival Masks Display

Festivals are the expression of celebrated religious life and nearly all faiths have a circle of festivals. Music and dance are a vital part of most festivals, many having their own particular type of music associated with them. The word 'carnival' comes from the Latin words meaning 'goodbye to meat', and originally carnivals were celebrated in countries where Roman Catholicism was the main faith. In most countries carnivals are held just before the period in the Christian year called Lent, where traditionally people gave up a food, such as meat.

Resources

- Jazz music
- Saxophone
- Combs, drums, sticks, bottles and tambourines
- Circular card
- Plastic masks
- Collage materials
- Paint, glue and scissors

Approach

1. Explain to the children the meaning of carnivals and that in New Orleans this celebration is called Mardi Gras (Fat Tuesday). The music of Mardi Gras is jazz.

2. Play some jazz music, for example music by Louis Armstrong, any New Orleans traditional Jazz music, or songs by King Oliver's Creole Jazz Band. Identify the instruments played, such as saxophone and trumpet. Most jazz is improvised and jazz musicians almost never play a tune the same way twice. Discuss the characteristics of jazz, the relaxed style and catchy rhythms.

3. If possible, display a saxophone and arrange for a saxophonist to play to the children.

4. Explain how the Mardi Gras musicians often use combs, drums, sticks, bottles and tambourines to play distinctive sounds. Experiment creating sounds using these instruments and materials. Talk about how the leaders sing out a line of a song and the rest of the group sing back the reply. This is called 'call and response'. Listen to examples, such as *Bear in the Woods* and *Tongo*, which can both be listened to on the Internet.

5. Talk to the children about Mardi Gras masks. Provide plastic masks for each child to sketch a design on.

6. Stick plastic masks onto circular pieces of card and use the collage materials to decorate the carnival masks.

Yellow Bird Display

Resources

- Calypso music
- Maracas
- Large sheet of card
- Feathers
- Paint and brushes

Approach

1. Give the children the opportunity to listen to some calypsos from the *Calypso Holiday* album (Collectables, 1999), for example *Yellow Bird* (1957) by The Norman Luboff Choir. Explain that calypsos are songs which originated in the West Indies. They are frequently improvised and the lyrics of calypsos are humorous and witty, and often about political themes or social and economic issues. Point out that calypsos are generally sung to a guitar and maracas, but more recently steel drums have also been used.

2. Discuss how, during carnival time, singers will meet in carnival halls called 'tents' and sing calypsos to compete for the title of king or queen. The most popular calypso becomes the theme of the carnival and is chosen as the carnival song.

3. Listen again to the calypso *Yellow Bird*.
   Encourage the children to sing along to the lyrics and provide maracas to accompany the song.

4. Ask the children to imagine *Yellow Bird* has won the calypso competition and design an outfit for the carnival king or queen to wear based on this song.

5. Children should first sketch out their design, then paint it and add different-coloured feathers.

Fireworks

George Frideric Handel (1685–1759) was born in Germany, trained in Italy and lived and worked in England for various Princes and Dukes. He is one of the most famous composers of the Baroque era. Baroque is a word to describe a new style of music and art, which emerged between 1600 and 1750. Baroque paintings and architecture were very ornate and the music echoed this. Handel is known mainly as the composer of the *Water Music*, *Music for the Royal Fireworks* and *Messiah*. *Music for the Royal Fireworks* was composed to celebrate a peace treaty and the occasion called for outdoor music. At the public rehearsal of the music, one hundred musicians played to an audience of more than 12 000. The fireworks themselves were a disappointment and even started a fire, burning down a park pavilion!

Resources

- *Music for the Royal Fireworks* by Handel
- Black card
- Matchsticks
- Brightly-coloured paints
- Wax pastels
- Sequins and glue

Approach

1. One of the most distinctive features of Baroque music is its instrumentation. Play *Music for the Royal Fireworks* by Handel and ask the children to identify some of the instruments: horns, trumpets, harpsichord and so on. Tell the children the story behind the composition of the 'firework music' and ask them to imagine the scene at the public rehearsal.

2. Give each child a sheet of black card, a selection of brightly-coloured paints and pastels and a matchstick. Ask the children to recreate a firework night sky using a mixture of pastel patterns, paint and sequins. Demonstrate how to apply the paint using the end of a matchstick to create stars and swirling patterns.

3. Discuss what instruments could be used to make the sounds of fireworks.

Cross-curricular Links

SCIENCE: Handel was born in 1685. In 1687 Isaac Newton developed the theory of gravity. Find out more about gravity.

LITERACY: Read extracts from *The Firework-Maker's Daughter* by Philip Pullman (Doubleday, 1995).

HISTORY: Research the gunpowder plot and the reign of James I.

Chinese Dragon

The fifth month of the Chinese year is traditionally associated with the dragon; the fifth day of the fifth month is a particularly important day. On this day the dragon boat races take place and the boats often have a dragon head carved on the front. The event commemorates the poet Chu Yuen who drowned himself to highlight the corrupt Emperor's policies. Chu Yuen was a very popular man and the local villagers are said to have taken to their boats and distracted the fish from eating his body by throwing rice into the water.

Resources

- Chinese festival music
- PVA glue
- Withie canes
- Masking tape
- Sponges
- Tissue paper
- Collage material
- Drums, cymbals and gongs

Approach

1. Listen to some Chinese festival music, such as *Chinese New Year Music* by Heart of the Dragon (ARC, 2007), and encourage the children to identify the sound of the drums, cymbals and gongs. Talk about how dragons feature quite prominently in another Chinese festival – the Chinese New Year.

2. To make a Chinese dragon, soak the withie canes in water for an hour or so to make them pliable. Bend the cane into a dragon head and secure together with masking tape.

3. Make a mix of PVA glue and water in a bowl and use a sponge to carefully cover a sheet of tissue with the glue. Drape the tissue paper over the withie structure. Cover with another layer of PVA mixture so that the tissue dries hard.

4. Embellish with collage material.

5. Provide drums, cymbals and gongs and encourage the children to explore sounds and create a short musical piece to accompany a performance of a dragon dance using the withie structure.

Cross-curricular Links

HISTORY: Explore the concept of martyrdom; discuss why people would be prepared to die for a cause they felt extremely strongly about.

LITERACY: Read stories about dragons from myths and legends, such as *The Dragon New Year: A Chinese Legend* by David Bouchard (Peachtree, 1999).

© Leisa Johnson/Corbis

Imagine Display

Resources

- *Imagine* by John Lennon
- Copy of *Imagine* lyrics
- Cartridge paper
- Paint, crayons and brushes

The 1960s heralded a new generation of musicians, many of whom were passionately involved in political activities and had dreams and hopes for a fairer, more peaceful world. A lot of musicians of this time produced songs with powerful messages, which became anthems for peace protesting against war and social injustice.

Approach

1. Listen to the song *Imagine* by John Lennon (Parlophone, 1999). Ask the children to listen for key phrases and write them down. Introduce the term 'lyrics'.

2. Discuss with the children what John Lennon was asking us to imagine and how the repetition of this word contributes to the mood of the song.

3. The lyrics tell us Lennon's idea of a perfect world, a utopia where everyone lives in peace. The song claims that love can conquer all and for a lot of people it epitomised the whole hippy movement of the 1960s and '70s.

4. Listen again to the song and identify the main instrument (piano). Ask the children how the vocals and lack of other musical instruments contribute to the mood of the song. Ask the children how they feel when listening to the lyrics and rhythm of the song … upbeat and hopeful, or reflective and thoughtful?

5. Look at the structure of the verses; identify rhyming patterns and where phrases have been repeated. Challenge the children to write a new verse reflecting upon current global issues which they feel angry or disturbed about, for example, 'imagine there's no famine…'.

6. Give children a piece of paper in the shape of a head and ask them to visually interpret John Lennon's song or create a picture of their own utopia.

I'd Like to Teach the World to Sing

The song *I'd Like to Teach the World to Sing* by The New Seekers, was conceived in 1971 by an advertising agency for the Coca-Cola company. They were en route to London when heavy fog forced their plane to land at Shannon airport in Ireland. The passengers all had to share rooms at the only available hotel or camp out at the airport, and tempers ran high! The following morning the passengers were laughing and sharing their stories of their experiences over bottles of Coke and the advertising executives suddenly saw Coke as more than just a drink; they felt it was, in a small way, a common bond linking people together and this inspired the lyrics of a song depicting global unity. The advertisement struck a chord deeper than the normal response to an advertising campaign and the composers were asked to re-write the lyrics without reference to Coke to enable the song to be played on the radio.

Resources

- *I'd Like to Teach the World to Sing* by The New Seekers
- Copy of lyrics
- Card and collage materials
- Glue and scissors

Approach

1. Give the children a copy of the lyrics to the song *I'd Like to Teach the World to Sing* by The New Seekers and explore how the melody reflects the lyric. Does the repetition of certain lines make the words and melody easier to remember?

2. Ask the children to think about the psychology of advertising; how adverts are designed to be easily remembered and linked to a product. Discuss how successful this song is and why.

3. Ask the children to think about other adverts and associated songs, and explain why they think they work well.

4. Study the song and discuss what elements could be included in a visual interpretation of the lyrics.

5. Give the children card and collage materials to produce a picture of a person – real or imagined – from anywhere in the world.

6. Display all the children's individual collages around a picture of the world.

Cross-curricular Links

PSHCE: Discuss why the lyrics of the Coke advertisement had such an impact on the public. Explain how the composers were linking Coke to the idea of a common connection among people all over the world. Ask each child to think of one thing that they think they have in common with all other children in the world; it could be something they enjoy doing or a basic need. Collate all ideas together in the form of a poster.

Peace Doves Display

Resources

- *Give Peace a Chance* by John Lennon
- Copy of *Dove of Peace* by Pablo Picasso
- Collage materials
- Scissors and glue

The song *Give Peace a Chance* was recorded in 1969 by John Lennon and Yoko Ono at the famous 'bed in' to promote peace. During the 'bed in' a reporter asked John Lennon what he was trying to do and spontaneously he said 'All we are saying is give peace a chance'. He liked the phrase and subsequently set it to music. *Give Peace a Chance* has since become a peace anthem and is often sung at protests.

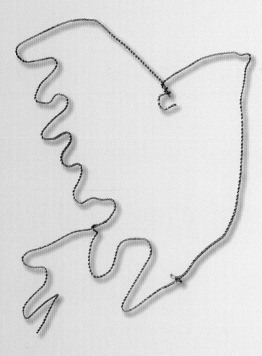

Approach

1. Listen to the song *Give Peace a Chance* by John Lennon. Discuss whether the message of the song is one of peace. Ask the children if they think it is still relevant today and why.

2. Talk about visual images of peace, especially the dove symbol. Look at the work by Pablo Picasso entitled *Dove of Peace* (1957).

3. Offer the children a choice of art materials, including: wire, felt, coloured card and sequins. Using Picasso's *Dove of Peace* as inspiration, ask the children to produce their own dove of peace picture.

4. Display all the different pictures together as one large dove of peace display.

Cross-curricular Links

LITERACY: Write poems entitled 'Peace'.

Adinkra Cloth Designs

Resources

- Recording of *Kumbayah*
- Lyrics of *Kumbayah*
- Copy of *Declaration of Human Rights*
- Pictures of Adinkra symbols and cloth
- Small piece of cloth
- Fabric paint and brushes

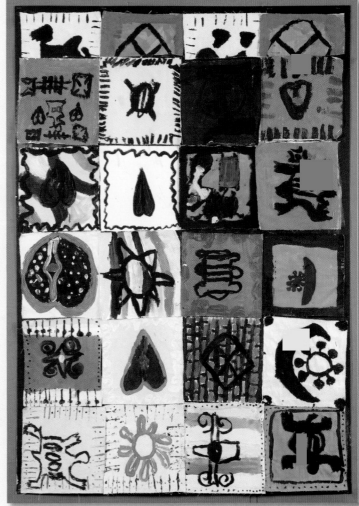

Approach

1. Listen to the song *Kumbayah*. Explain that Kumbayah means 'come by here' in the Gullah dialect. The Gullah people live in the region of Georgia and South Carolina; these islanders have a strong connection with African culture within their music, language and traditions. Although open to debate, it is generally agreed that the origins of this song came from the Gullah people who had converted to Christianity in the 19th century. In 1962 Joan Baez recorded the song and it became associated with the Civil Rights movement.

   Kumbayah is a traditional African-American spiritual. Explain that spirituals are Christian songs concerned with teachings of the Bible and how to live within the spirit of God.

2. Discuss the *Declaration of Human Rights* (there is an adapted version for children published by the United Nations). Ask each child to focus on one particular declaration and incorporate it into a new verse for *Kumbayah*, set to the same format and musical composition.

3. Discuss how, before 1865, almost all the first Africans who arrived in the New World were slaves. Ask the children to imagine the emotions of the African slaves; their hopes, fears and memories of their homeland, and write them down.

4. Look at Adinkra patterned cloth, which is made using a traditional African method of decoration with symbols that convey the thoughts and feelings of the people wearing them.

5. Study the Adinkra symbols and ask the children to make up their own symbol to represent a feeling, hope or dream of the African slaves who first sang *Kumbayah*.

6. Paint onto fabric and display as an Adinkra quilt, putting all the children's ideas together.

Cross-curricular Links

HISTORY: Look at the Civil Rights movement and Martin Luther King's role. Discuss why *Kumbayah* had a revival at this time.

LITERACY: Look at the famous speech by Martin Luther King … '*I have a dream …*' and ask the children to prepare a similar speech focusing on the fight for equality in all areas of life that people face in the 21st century.

Four Seasons Violin Display

Resources

- *The Four Seasons* by Antonio Vivaldi
- Copies of Vivaldi's *Four Seasons Sonnets*
- Percussion instruments
- Card
- Silk and gutta
- Silk paints and brushes

The Four Seasons by Antonio Vivaldi (1678–1741) was written in 1726. The music is a series of four short concertos. A concerto is a piece of music in which a single instrument (in this case, violin) is accompanied by an orchestra. Most concertos have three sections; quick, slow, quick. Vivaldi was a leading composer of Baroque music and wrote over 500 concertos, many for the orchestra and choir at a girls' orphanage where he worked. *The Four Seasons* is an early example of programme music, which is a piece of music that has been especially composed to create the mood of a picture or a poem, or tell a story.

Approach

1. Listen to extracts of *The Four Seasons*. Explain the meaning of a concerto and that this is an example of a violin concerto. Discuss the ways in which the sounds have been used to create the mood of the seasons. For example, how has Vivaldi portrayed the different types of weather?

2. Using a variety of percussion instruments, experiment with creating sounds to reflect the different seasons.

3. Explain that when the music was originally performed, each movement was preceded by a sonnet (a poem). Read Vivaldi's sonnets to the class and discuss how these help to build up the sound picture of the seasons in each movement.

4. Cut out templates of violins. Provide silk and silk paints for the children to create seasonal pictures. Encourage the children to 'draw' with the gutta first and fill in the areas with the paint. The gutta will prevent the silk paint from spreading.

5. Ask the children to write some sonnets using the seasons for inspiration.

6. Display the violin pictures and the sonnets together.

Four Seasons Tree Display

Resources

- *The Four Seasons* by Antonio Vivaldi
- Variety of instruments
- Large sheet of card
- Paint and brushes
- Collage materials

Approach

1. Listen again to extracts from Vivaldi's *The Four Seasons*. Ask the children to describe how each concerto made them feel and identify which season each one portrayed.

2. Discuss the effects of changing seasons on nature. Ask the children to visualise the changing image of a tree throughout the four seasons. Encourage the children to talk about things that happen to a tree throughout the changing year. Provide the children with a variety of instruments and help them invent sounds to represent each phase of the changing seasons for the tree.

3. Provide a large sheet of card for each group of four children, and ask them to draw a tree covering the card.

4. Divide the card into four sections and ask each child to choose a season and paint their part accordingly. Provide collage materials such as glitter and snowflakes for the winter section.

5. Using the display as inspiration, ask each group of children to compose their own seasonal sounds taking the audience through the changing four seasons.

Spring Blossom Pictures

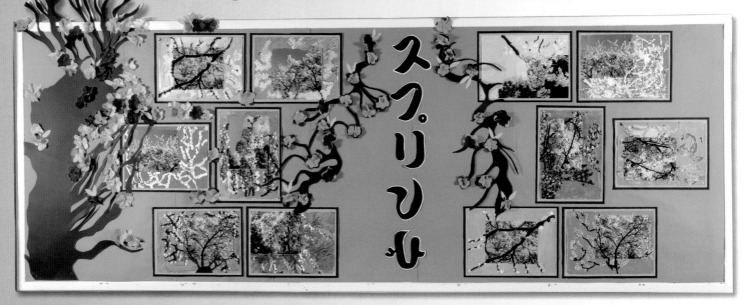

Approach

1. Listen to the *Spring Concerto* from *The Four Seasons*. Encourage the children to identify the birdsong, the spring storm and the village dance in the third movement.

2. Discuss what instruments have been used to create the different sounds and allow the children to experiment making their own spring sounds, such as that of birdsong.

3. Look at how spring is depicted in art. Encourage the children to look at work by various artists that clearly portray the season of spring, such as *In a Shoreham Garden* by Samuel Palmer (1805–81), *The Seine at la Grande Jatte in the Spring* by George Seurat (1859–91) or *Plum Trees in Blossom Outside the Tea House at Kameido (after Hiroshige)* by Vincent van Gogh (1853–90).

4. Encourage the children to study the different ways blossom has been portrayed in these pictures.

5. Take photographs of spring blossom and give each child a copy stuck onto a larger sheet of paper.

6. Provide paint for the children to create blossom pictures, referring to the different techniques of the various artists' examples.

7. Display the work as a tree, with card branches and apple blossom made out of scrunched-up tissue paper.

Resources

- *The Four Seasons* by Antonio Vivaldi
- Examples of Van Gogh's Japanese woodcuts
- Examples of art depicting spring
- Photographs of spring blossom
- Paint and brushes
- Tissue paper

Cross-curricular Links

RE: Read 'for everything there is a season' from *The Book of Ecclesiastes* (The Bible). Discuss the meaning of the verse and listen to *Turn! Turn! Turn! (To Everything There is a Season)* by Judy Collins (the lyrics are taken from *The Book of Ecclesiastes*).

Summer based on **Miró**

Resources

- *The Four Seasons* by Antonio Vivaldi
- Pictures of *Summer* by Joan Miró
- Sheets of coloured paper
- Scissors, glue and cartridge paper

Approach

1. Listen to the *Summer Concerto* from *The Four Seasons* by Antonio Vivaldi and discuss with the children memories of summer holidays. Ask if there are any particular sounds or smells they relate to summer.

2. Look at the work of Joan Miró (1893–1983) entitled *Summer*. Miró was a leading Spanish surrealist and admired the spontaneous freedom and expression of children. Discuss the strange life forms he has created. Can the children 'feel' the heat of the Mediterranean sun through Miró's choice of colour?

3. Using their own memories and images of summer, the children could create a summer collage.

Autumn based on **van Gogh**

Resources

- *The Four Seasons* by Antonio Vivaldi
- Copies of Vivaldi's *Four Seasons Sonnets*
- Pictures of autumn harvests by van Gogh
- Cartridge paper and tea bags
- Ink pens and sepia inks

Approach

1. Listen to the *Autumn Concerto* from *The Four Seasons* by Antonio Vivaldi.

2. Read the sonnet and discuss how it refers to the joy of gathering a bountiful harvest – a powerful image of autumn time.

3. Look at harvest artwork by Vincent van Gogh (1853–90), such as *Harvest in Provence* (1888), which show fields of autumn corn and harvests. Discuss his use of lines and how it suggests the movement of the corn in the autumn wind.

4. Allow the children to experiment with mark making: dots, slashes, lines, wavy lines and so on to see what effects can be made.

5. Use wet tea bags to stain pieces of cartridge paper.

6. When the paper has dried, use pens and sepia-coloured ink to create a harvest picture in the style of van Gogh.

Cross-curricular Links

RE: Study the Christian harvest festival. Make corn dollies from straw or painted drinking straws.

Planets Display

The *Planets Suite* was written between 1914 and 1916 by Gustav Holst (1874–1934). The suite is devoted to seven planets and the traditional order of performance is Mars, Venus, Mercury, Jupiter, Saturn, Uranus and Neptune. Pluto doesn't feature, as this planet wasn't discovered until 1930.

Resources

- *Planets Suite* by Gustav Holst
- Pictures of planets and space
- Card and glue
- Paint and brushes
- Collage material
- Variety of instruments

Approach

1. Explain to the children that a suite is a collection of instrumental pieces designed to be played one after another. Gustav Holst drew upon his knowledge of astrology and mythology to compose the *Planets Suite*. Ask the children to research a particular planet and report back to the class.

2. Listen to extracts of the *Planets Suite* and discuss the ways that Holst has interpreted the characteristics of each planet musically, for example, contrast the aggression of Mars with the serenity of Saturn. Discuss how the planets in our solar system have acquired emotional characteristics, for example, Mars and war.

3. Look at pictures of the planets and space, and explore ideas of what it might be like to go on a space journey. Does the mood of the music reflect their emotions? Provide a variety of instruments and ask the children to explore sounds that create a feeling of travelling through endless space.

4. With the children working in groups, ask them to visually interpret the planet of their choice. Provide a variety of collage material and focus the children on the distinguishing features of their particular planet.

5. When the solar system is complete, ask the children to use their knowledge of their particular planet to make up a musical sequence depicting its characteristics.

6. Combine the musical sequences together in the order of the *Planets Suite* (see display above).

Big Bang Display

Approach

1. Explain to the children the concept of the 'big bang' theory.

2. Discuss the sounds and instruments that could be used to interpret this event musically.

3. Talk about the images surrounding the big bang. Provide the children with a black sheet of paper. Ask them to use straws to blow paint into explosive shapes and use their fingers to spread the paint.

4. Embellish with glitter and sequins.

Resources

- Black card
- Bright coloured paint
- Glitter, sequins and straws

Cross-curricular Links

LITERACY: Look at the famous poem (hymn) set to *Jupiter* from Holst's *Planets Suite*. The first verse was played at the wedding of Prince Charles and Lady Diana and its second verse was sung at Princess Diana's funeral in 1997.

Solar System Silk Paintings

Approach

1. Listen to extracts of the *Planets Suite* by Gustav Holst. Encourage the children to close their eyes and imagine the journey through space that the music takes them on. Discuss these images, colours and shapes.

2. Give groups of children a piece of silk. Divide the silk into sections using gutta. The children should fill each area with images of space.

3. When the gutta is dry, paint with silk paints.

Resources

- *Planets Suite* by Gustav Holst
- Large pieces of silk
- Silk paints and gutta

Cross-curricular Links

ICT: Ask the children to find out more about space and planets by visiting the NASA website: science.hq.nasa.gov/.

SCIENCE: Study the part the moon plays in our solar system. Study the phases of the moon and keep a diary of how it changes shape. The moon is a satellite of the Earth; it is not a planet and it is approximately 385 000km away from the Earth. It takes approximately 28 days to orbit the Earth.

HISTORY: Study the first 'man on the moon' landing in 1969. Write a newspaper report of this event.

Lunar Surface Display

Resources

- Percussion instruments
- Photographic paper
- Three plastic trays
- Developer and fixer
- Tongs and brushes
- Balloons
- Papier mâché
- Paint
- Mod roc
- Large sheet of card

Approach

1. Talk about the moon's place in our solar system and how, even though it doesn't feature in the *Planets Suite*, it has been the subject of many musical compositions. Examples of listening music include *Fly me to the Moon* by Frank Sinatra and *Moon River* by Andy Williams. Discuss the first moon landing and imagine sounds that would portray the scene: the weightlessness, the barren landscape, the feeling of awe and so on.

2. Encourage the children to create a sequence of sounds using percussion instruments that would tell the story of the first moon landing: the rocket landing, the first step, putting up the flag and so on. Explore ways of bringing the sounds together.

3. Work together to make photographic images. Fill one plastic tray with water. Following the instructions on the bottles, mix the developer with water in the second tray, and mix the fixer with water in the third tray.

4. Explain to the children about the qualities of photographic paper – once it is exposed to light it will start to react and colour. It is important to caution them about using chemicals. Although perfectly safe if handled correctly, chemicals must not go near the eyes or mouth.

5. Remove a sheet of photographic paper from its black bag and paint a lunar surface using a paintbrush dipped in developer.

6. Using tongs, submerge the paper into the fixer for about five minutes.

7. Remove and put in the final tray of water for at least ten minutes. Dry flat.

8. Display with a lunar surface of papier mâché balloons attached to card with mod roc, then painted.

Tie Dye Suns and Stars

Resources

- Picture of *Starry Night* by Vincent van Gogh
- *Starry Starry Night* by Don McLean
- Pieces of cotton fabric
- Yellow and purple dye
- Card
- Paint and brushes
- Elastic bands
- Silver collage material
- Dried peas or marbles
- Iron

Approach

1. Show the children *Starry Night* (1889) by Vincent van Gogh and tell the children this artwork inspired the song *Starry Starry Night;* play Don McLean's version while the children work.

2. Give each child a square piece of fabric. To create circular patterns, they should place some dried peas or marbles on the fabric and secure in place by twisting an elastic band around the fabric. Encourage the children to twist the bands on tightly to stop the dye reaching this part of the cloth.

3. Give the children a choice as to whether their cloth is going to be a sun or a star picture and dye accordingly.

4. Remove the squares from the dye, rinse them, and leave to dry.

5. When dry, untie the squares and iron them.

6. Cut the yellow ones into circles and give the children paper and paints to make their cloth into a sun.

7. Leave the purple ones square and provide the children with silver collage materials (such as stars and sequins) to embellish their designs.

The Three Musicians

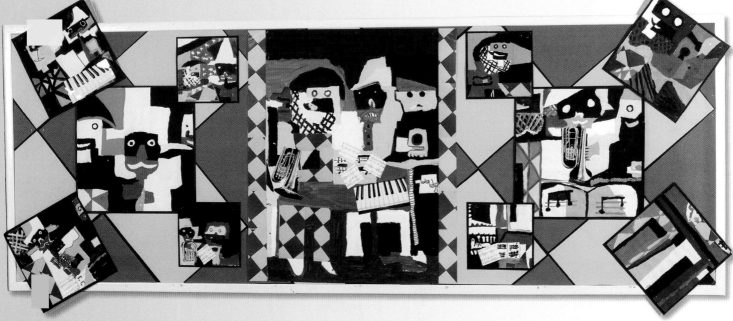

Musicians and their instruments have been a fascinating subject for painters for thousands of years. Often a painter will try to capture the mood of the instrument and music that is being played; for example delicate and gentle colour schemes may indicate soothing melodic music. Other times a strong feeling of rhythm may be expressed by vibrant colours and bold shapes.

Resources

- Picture of *The Three Musicians* by Pablo Picasso
- Viewfinders
- Pictures of musical instruments
- Paint and brushes
- Cartridge paper

Approach

1. Show the children a copy of *The Three Musicians* by Pablo Picasso, painted in 1921. Pablo Picasso was born in Spain, the son of an art teacher, and was one of the greatest artists of the 20th century. Along with George Braque, Picasso invented a new style of art called 'Cubism' where the objects or people appear to be jumbled up and broken into a flat pattern of geometric shapes.

2. Encourage the children to identify the three musicians and the instruments they are playing, which include a violin and a clarinet. Ask the children to 'listen' to the picture and talk about the music they might hear.

3. Ask the children to focus on a small part of the picture by using a viewfinder to isolate interesting sections.

4. Ask the children to enlarge their chosen section onto a sheet of cartridge paper, then paint and use collage pictures of instruments to add to the texture.

The Three Musicians (1921) by Pablo Picasso
© Philadelphia Museum of Art / CORBIS

Pierrot the Musician

Gino Severini (1883–1966) was a member of the Italian Futurists, a group of artists who rejected the past and celebrated the dynamism of the machine age and city life. However, *Pierrot the Musician* (1924) marks the artist's movement away from the influence of futurism. He painted several compositions of theatrical artists with instruments, including *Two Punchinellos* (1922).

Resources

- Pictures of *Pierrot the Musician* by Gino Severini
- Cartridge paper
- Plastic masks
- Paint and brushes
- Collage material

Pierrot the Musician, 1924, Severini, Gino (1883–1966) © ADAGP, Paris and DACS / Museum Boymans van Beuningen, Rotterdam, The Netherlands / The Bridgeman Art Library, London 2007

Approach

1. Discuss the composition of *Pierrot the Musician*. Ask the children to focus on Severini's use of colour and pattern. What mood does this help to create? Ask the children to imagine the musician playing the guitar; what music could they hear?

2. Talk about how Severini has portrayed the stiff folds of Pierrot's outfit and demonstrate how this could be achieved in a 3-D way by folding and rolling paper.

3. Give each child a plastic mask and ask them to create a 3-D version of Pierrot in paper sculpture and collage, finishing with paint.

The Green Violinist

Marc Chagall (1887–1985) was a Russian artist. He painted *The Green Violinist* in 1923, originally for the theatre, to symbolise the art of music. His style was to blend reality and dreams into colourful compositions. He painted as though life were a fairy tale.

Resources

- *Music (Jewish Theatre)* 1923 by Marc Chagall
- Violin
- Cartridge paper
- Paint
- Pictures of violins
- *Violin Concerto in D Major* by Ludwig van Beethoven

Music (Jewish Theatre), 1923 (tempera, gouache and white clay on canvas), Chagall, Marc (1887–1985) © ADAGP Paris and DACS London 2007 / Tretyakov Gallery, Moscow, Russia / The Bridgeman Art Library

Approach

1. Discuss the composition of *Music (Jewish Theatre)* 1923 by Marc Chagall, otherwise known as 'The Green Violinist'. Why has he painted the musician's face green? Could it be to provide a theatrical effect? Why is Chagall's fiddler floating high above the village? The Jewish culture in which he was raised told Hassidic legends where people fly, trees laugh and there are fiddlers on the rooftops; the influence of these stories feature in many of his works.

2. Show the children a violin and if possible allow them to hear it being played. Ask the children if they think the choice of instrument is an important aspect of the painting and, if so, why. What kind of tune would the violinist be playing?

3. Provide the children with a picture of a violin and ask them to create their own version of 'The Green Violinist' using lively designs based on geometric shapes. Children could listen to background music as they work, such as Ludwig van Beethoven's *Violin Concerto in D Major*.

Cubist Still Life

The term 'cubism', like 'impressionism' before it, was a label coined by a less than complimentary art critic. It had its roots in the work of Paul Cézanne, whose subject matter was landscape, but the main pioneers were Pablo Picasso and George Braque. Cubism breaks down real objects into different parts and cubist artists explored the contradictory concept of portraying three-dimensional objects on a two-dimensional surface.

Resources

- Examples of cubist still life pictures
- Objects to create a still life composition
- Coloured paper
- Graphite pencils, chalk
- Collage materials
- Scissors and glue

Approach

1. Explain to the children that a still life picture is a picture of everyday objects carefully chosen and placed in an arrangement. A lot of cubist artists used instruments in their still life arrangements. Examples include: *Clarinet and Bottle of Rum* by George Braque (1911), *Guitar and Clarinet* by Juan Gris (1920), *Guitar and Mandolin (The Open Window)* by Pablo Picasso (1923) and *Violin Hanging on the Wall* by Pablo Picasso (1913). Very often the elements of the composition are taken apart and reassembled in ways which focus attention on the musical instruments. Ask the children to name the instruments in the examples and any other objects they can identify.

Guitar and Clarinet 1920 (oil on canvas) Gris, Juan (1887–1927)
© Kunstmuseum, Basel, Switzerland /The Bridgeman Art Library

2. Make an arrangement of still life objects, including musical instruments, and allow the children to study the composition by moving around it and choosing a place to sit and draw.

3. Ask the children to make several quick sketches of the arrangement, changing places for each drawing. Provide a variety of drawing materials: chalks, pencils and so on. Encourage the children initially to make their drawings as representational as possible.

4. Ask the children to look at their drawings and think of their picture in terms of 3-D shapes, as if they are viewing the objects from the back as well as the front. Encourage them to simplify the forms and make them disjointed. Use coloured paper, fragments of painted paper, music paper and collage material of all kinds to produce a cubist still life picture.

Carnival of the Animals Wood Picture

The *Carnival of the Animals* was written by the French composer Camille Saint-Saëns (1835–1921). The light-hearted zoological fantasy was written as a surprise gift for a cellist friend. Saint-Saëns was concerned that the less-than-serious music was too frivolous to be published, and after a concert in 1886 he refused to allow it to be played again. The *Carnival of the Animals* consists of 14 short movements and most are linked to a particular animal with the exceptions being the *Fossils* and *Pianists* movements.

Resources

- *Carnival of the Animals* by Camille Saint-Saëns
- Large sheet of plywood
- Collection of wood: shavings, sawdust, chippings
- Sheet of card
- Glue and glue spreaders

Approach

1. Play the *Carnival of the Animals* by Camille Saint-Saëns (EMI Classics, 2001); stop after each movement and ask the children which animal they associate with the music. Provide a list of all the animals featured so the children can link the music to each animal. Encourage the children to explore the musical features: how does the music help us imagine how the animals behave and move? Point out that the musical sounds differ according to each animal's distinctive characteristics. Ask them to predict what sounds, instruments and tempos they think a particular movement will be like; for example, for the *March of the Lions*, play the movement, identify the instruments and compare notes.

2. Provide a list of all the featured animals and ask the children to choose one to draw and sculpt in wood.

3. Provide a collection of wood shavings, sawdust, chippings and so on. Encourage the children to explore the different qualities of the wood pieces, looking at texture, colour and shape.

4. Ask the children to sketch out their chosen animal on a piece of card, cut it out and use the wood pieces to create a 3-D collage of their animal.

5. Display all the animals on a large sheet of plywood.

Cross-curricular Links

LITERACY: Write poems to accompany the different animals in Saint-Saëns' music. If possible, refer to the ones in the published book *The Carnival of the Animals* (Book & CD), (Walker Books, 2005).

Tortoise Picture

Resources

- *Carnival of the Animals* by Camille Saint-Saëns
- Balloons
- Papier mâché
- Paint and brushes
- Variety of percussion instruments

Approach

1. Play the *Tortoises* movement from *Carnival of the Animals* to the class. Ask them to close their eyes and imagine the creatures. The tortoises dance to the cancan during this movement. Prompt the children to listen out for this popular tune.

2. Ask the children to collect ideas about how a tortoise would move, what it looks like, its size, its age, natural environment and so on. Explain how these ideas can be presented in the form of a poem and demonstrate a suitable format. Encourage the children to write their own group versions. They should then consider the most appropriate instruments to create background sound to perform their poem to. Provide a variety of percussion instruments and allow the children to experiment with rhythm and melodies.

3. Blow up the balloons (one per pair of children). Ask the children to paper maché at least two layers. When dry, cut in half.

4. Using their research on tortoises, the children can sketch out designs of tortoise shells onto the papier mâché.

5. Paint and display the tortoises on a large board.

6. Using the display as a background, ask the children to perform their musical sound poems to the rest of the class.

Cross-curricular Links

LITERACY: Read stories about tortoises, such as *The Hare & the Tortoise: (Favourite Animal Fables)* (Chrysalis Books, 1993) and *Esio Trot* by Roald Dahl (Puffin Fiction, 2001).

Mosaic Aquarium

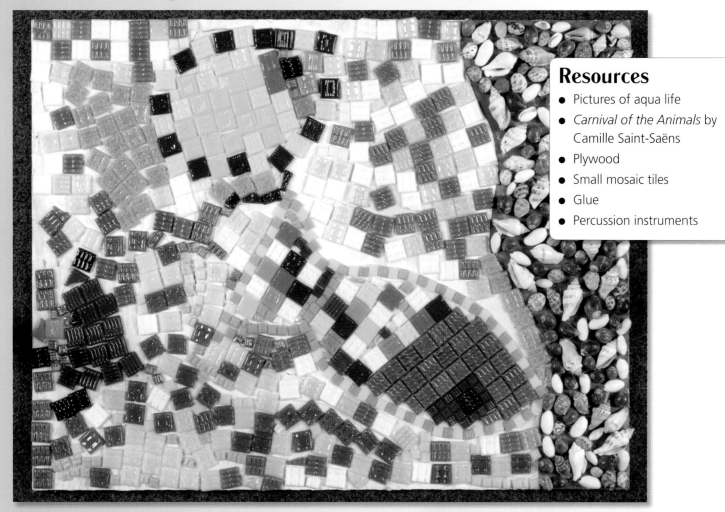

© Thinkstock / Corbis

Resources

- Pictures of aqua life
- *Carnival of the Animals* by Camille Saint-Saëns
- Plywood
- Small mosaic tiles
- Glue
- Percussion instruments

Approach

1. Play the *Aquarium* movement from *Carnival of the Animals* to the class. Ask the children what water images are evoked in their minds. Discuss the types of instruments used to create these images and ask them if they can think of any other instruments that could be used to make 'watery' music. Ask them which part they liked best, found most interesting, and what they thought of the beginning and the end.

2. Provide instruments and discuss what would be a good instrument to make the sound of the fish swimming in the aquarium. Encourage the children to listen out for the piano which provides the rippling sounds (in the *Aquarium* movement) and try to identify sounds linked to particular images, such as bubbles.

3. Study pictures of aqua life, concentrating on the shapes and bright colours of tropical fish.

4. Working together, the class could sketch out designs of an aquarium on paper, transfer to wood and cover in appropriately coloured mosaic tiles. If preferred, paper mosaic pieces can provide a similar effect on card.

Ugly Bug Ball

Resources

- *The Ugly Bug Ball – Summer Magic* by Disney
- Balloons
- Papier mâché
- Glue
- Paint and brushes
- Collage material
- Percussion instruments

Approach

1. Play Disney's *The Ugly Bug Ball – Summer Magic* to the children and discuss the lyrics (which can be printed from the Internet) and the images the song evokes.

2. Ask the class to work in pairs, choose an insect and create sounds and movements to describe their insect. Using instruments, ask the children to work out a sequence of sounds and movements and perform to the rest of the class. Ask the class to guess the insect each pair is portraying.

3. Ask the children to sketch out an imaginary insect attending the ugly bug ball. The insect can have features of one or more creatures and be as imaginatively ugly as they like.

4. Blow up the balloons (one per pair of children). Ask the children to papier mâché at least two layers. When dry, cut in half. Decorate as 3-D ugly bugs. Use brightly-coloured paint and collage material (such as pipe cleaners).

Cross-curricular Links

SCIENCE: Research mini beasts and write fact files about real bugs to display alongside the ugly bugs.

MUSIC: Listen to the *Flight of the Bumble Bee* by Nikolai Rimsky-Korsakov (1844–1908) and research the story behind the music.

I Am the Music Man

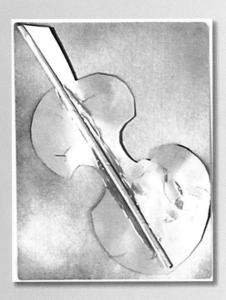

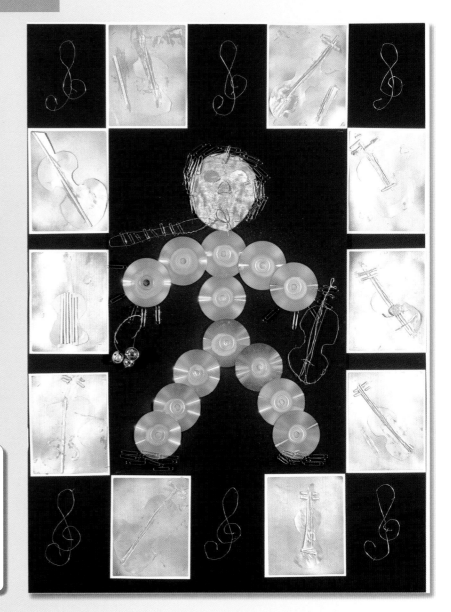

Resources

- *I Am the Music Man* song
- Wire/metal collage material
- Old CDs
- Large sheets of card
- Percussion instruments

Approach

1. Introduce the children to the well-known song *I Am the Music Man* (music and lyrics can be found on the Internet). It is an action song that incorporates many different instruments. Make a list of all the instruments that could be included in the song and if possible arrange for the children to hear the range of sounds of each one. Discuss how the sounds are made: by blowing, vibrating strings and tapping.

2. Look at the song again and ask the children if there are any lines which could be illustrated by a sound effect either by the actual instruments or using voices.

3. Provide groups of children with large sheets of card, wire, metal collage materials (such as paper clips) and old CDs. Working in small groups, ask them to make a collage of the music man. Try to make some of the instruments in metal and attach to the card using a long-armed stapler.

Cross-curricular Links

LITERACY: Read *The Iron Man* and the sequel *The Iron Woman* by Ted Hughes (Faber Children's Books). Discuss the role of the sequel. Write a story entitled 'The Music Man'.

Ebony and Ivory

The piano was originally called the 'pianoforte', an Italian word meaning soft and loud. It works by pressing a key which operates a lever that raises a small felt covered hammer which hits the string for that note. An upright piano has the steel strings arranged vertically whereas in a grand piano they are horizontal. The earliest pianofortes were made in the early 1700s by Bartolomeo Christofori (1655–1731). The piano has the ability to play several notes all at once, giving it a huge range of expression.

Resources

- *The Entertainer* by Scott Joplin
- *Moonlight Sonata* by Ludwig van Beethoven
- Pictures of Johannes Vermeer's Virginal paintings
- *Ebony and Ivory* by Paul McCartney and Stevie Wonder
- *Ebony and Ivory* lyrics
- Black and white card
- Photographs of piano keys
- Scissors and glue

Approach

1. There are many pieces of music written for solo piano; listen to Beethoven's *Moonlight Sonata* (1801) or Scott Joplin's *The Entertainer* (1902).

2. Explain to the children how the piano works and, if possible, arrange for a piano to be played to them and for them to look inside the lid to see the workings of the instrument.

3. Discuss the history of the piano and show early paintings of this instrument, such as one of the many 'Virginal' paintings by Johannes Vermeer (1632–1675).

4. Listen to a recording of *Ebony and Ivory* peformed by Paul McCartney and Stevie Wonder and give the children a copy of the lyrics (written by Paul McCartney). Discuss the message behind the song. Why was the piano used to link the music and message? Why is the song called *Ebony and Ivory*?

5. Encourage the children to sing along with the recording.

6. Give the children copies of the photographed piano keys and some black and white card. Choose a piece of piano music to play to the children and ask them to interpret the mood and speed of the music visually, using the idea of the keys moving to the music.

Cross-curricular Links

PSHCE: Discuss the concept of people living together in harmony. What would the word *harmony* suggest about the way Paul McCartney wanted people to live? Discuss ways of making the classroom environment harmonious and draw up a charter for the class.

Stringed Instruments

There are many different string instruments that are played in various ways. Modern bowed string instruments are the culmination of many centuries of development. The one thing they all have in common is tightly stretched strings that vibrate to produce sound. The shorter the string, the higher the note. Sometimes the strings are plucked with the fingers, sometimes they are played with a bow and there is also a group of instruments that have their strings hit by beaters or hammers. String instruments include the violin, the viola, the cello, the double bass, the harp, the guitar and the lute.

Resources

- String instrument music
- Boxes and elastic bands
- Black card
- String
- Glue and scissors
- Silver spray
- Pictures of string instruments

Approach

1. Look at the pictures of string instruments. Explain how they produce sound and if possible make some stringed instruments using a wide range of materials (such as cardboard boxes and elastic bands).

2. Listen to the various sounds stringed instruments make and challenge the children to identify the different ones. Suitable examples include: Felix Mendelssohn's *Violin Concerto*, Edward Elgar's *Cello Concerto* or Pyotr Tchaikovsky's *Serenade for Strings.*

3. Give each child a piece of black card, string, glue and scissors. Provide a variety of string instruments (or pictures) for the children to study and make preliminary drawings.

4. Ask the children to transfer their drawings onto card and outline in string.

5. Cut out a large treble clef, pin to a display board and spray around it in silver spray.

6. Remove the treble clef and reveal the shape.

7. Display the string instruments, backed on silver paper.

Quilling Patterns of Notation

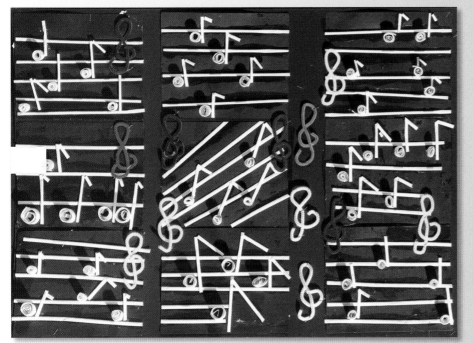

Notation is writing music down so that someone other than the original composer can play the music. In the ninth century, European monks would write a few signs in their prayer books to help them remember their holy songs and to indicate where voices should rise and fall. The early squiggles people used at the time didn't look much like music. In the eleventh century, a Benedictine monk and music teacher called Guido d'Arezzo placed marks on a grid of five lines called a stave, but it was another 500 years before people were writing music as we do today. The different symbols in the music stand for different lengths of time. The position of a note symbol, on a line or space, tells the pitch of the note – how high or low the note is.

Resources

- Quilling paper
- Glue
- Black card
- White art straws
- Pipe cleaners
- Recorders

Approach

1. Explain the three main points musicians need to know about musical sounds: how high or low the sounds are (pitch); how long or short the sounds are (rhythm) and how the music should be played (expression). Discuss the mixture of special signs and words that explain these things to the musician.

2. Explain that a clef is a sign used to explain which line means which note. There are two main clefs; the treble clef (for higher notes) and the bass clef (for lower notes). Look at the made up sentences which help us remember the names of the lines and spaces in each clef: F A C E (spaces) E G B D F (lines). Ask the children to make up their own silly sentences to help them remember the place of each note.

3. Demonstrate the art of quilling; rolling up long thin strips of quilling or cartridge paper and gluing at the end to create decorative designs.

4. Give the children art straws, quilling or cartridge paper and glue and ask them to design a piece of music using the spaces and lines as discussed previously. Children could use pipe cleaners to make a treble clef.

5. Challenge the children to play their quilling music on a recorder. Can they put several designs together and produce a larger piece of music?

The Snowman

Approach

1. Introduce the children to the story of *The Snowman* by Raymond Briggs (Picture Puffin, 2006). It is a wordless story where a little boy rushes out into his garden on a winter's day to make a snowman. The Snowman comes alive in his dreams that night and they embark on a magical adventure.

2. In 1982 Howard Blake wrote the words and music for *The Snowman,* which has since become a classic. In the film, the theme song *Walking in the Air* was sung by Peter Auty; this song was then released as a single, sung by Aled Jones and became world famous. If possible, play the song and arrange for the children to see the film.

3. Discuss the appeal of both the book and animated film. Ask the children what it is about the music that helps set the mood of the snow scenes and the excitement of the magical journey.

4. Blow up the balloons (one large and one small per pair of children). Ask the children to papier mâché at least two layers. When dry, cut in half and give each child one large half and one small half.

5. Attach the papier mâché to a piece of card using strips of paper and glue.

6. Paint white and decorate using a variety of collage material.

Resources

- *The Snowman* by Raymond Briggs
- *Walking in the Air* by Aled Jones
- *The Snowman* DVD
- Balloons and papier mâché
- Glue and scissors
- White paint
- Collage material

Cross-curricular Links

LITERACY: Provide copies of evocative winter poems. Encourage children to write their own poems and tunes to accompany them. Write some text to go with a small part of *The Snowman* story. Look carefully at the pictures and discuss what is happening, and what the little boy and the Snowman could be saying to each other.

Alice in Wonderland

Lewis Carroll's classic story *Alice's Adventures in Wonderland,* written in 1865 tells the story of a fantasy land inhabited by strange creatures and talking playing cards. One of the main themes of the story is parody and satire, and there are many examples of this related to nursery rhymes. For example *Twinkle Twinkle Little Bat* is a parody of *Twinkle Twinkle Little Star.*

Resources

- *Alice in Wonderland* DVD (1951)
- Percussion instruments
- Red, white and black card
- Scissors and glue
- Playing cards

Approach

1. If possible, play parts of Disney's animated fantasy version of *Alice in Wonderland.* Show how Disney interprets the blustering Queen of Hearts. The Disney film released in 1951 is a popular cinematic adaptation of the story. Look how Disney portrays the many different characters in the story: the White Rabbit, Mad Hatter and the Caterpillar as slightly psychedelic characters. Give the children a list of characters and ask them to visually interpret them in the style of Disney.

2. Discuss the character of the Queen of Hearts who screams 'off with his/her head' at anyone she feels slightly annoyed with. Look at the original 'Queen of Hearts' nursery rhyme and ask the children to rewrite it, thinking about the character Carroll portrays in his book.

3. Provide percussion instruments for the children to use to accompany the performance of their rhymes.

4. Look at the symbols on a pack of cards and make patterns in coloured card using one or more of the different playing suits.

5. Display alongside a queen of hearts made from card.

Cross-curricular Links

LITERACY: Explore the use of puns, parody and satire in poems and stories. Look at nonsense poems and encourage children to try writing their own versions. Explore the use of dreams and nightmares in stories. Ask the children to write their own dream or nightmare story. Print from the Internet Lewis Carroll's *Jabberwocky* poem (1871) and read to the class.

HISTORY: Look at the life of Queen Victoria who was among the first avid readers of *Alice's Adventures in Wonderland.*

Queen of Hearts

The queen of hearts
She made some tarts
'They're beautiful'
she beamed
The knave of hearts
He stole the tarts
'Off with his head'
she screamed!

by Lewis Carroll

The Snow Queen

Approach

1. Read the children *The Snow Queen* by Hans Christian Andersen (Templar Publishing, 2005). It is about two childhood friends, Kay and Gerda. When Kay is out playing one day he becomes ensnared by the Snow Queen who takes him to a bitterly cold palace deep in the frozen northern regions of the earth. She keeps Kay imprisoned there until his heart turns to ice. Gerda doesn't forget Kay and begins to search for her beloved friend, and – like all good fairy tales – they live happily ever after.

2. There are many musical interpretations of this story, including a version performed by The Royal Philharmonic Orchestra, and several ballets. If possible arrange for the children to experience parts of a musical interpretation of the story.

3. Discuss the character of the Snow Queen. Her great, frozen palace is vast, empty, glittering and icy cold. Give the children a variety of classroom instruments and ask them to experiment with sounds that capture the mood and character of the Snow Queen. Encourage them to find sounds which evoke feelings of the cold echoing loneliness of her palace. Read part of the story again and at the appropriate time, add in all the music and sounds the children have planned.

4. Give the children a sheet of paper and ask them to sketch out a design for the Snow Queen.

5. Provide a plastic mask and a sheet of card and provide a range of metallic collage materials, including glitter, tinsel, metallic papers and fabric. Allow time to explore the different collage materials, and demonstrate techniques to attach the mask to the card and make 3-D embellishments to the Snow Queen designs.

Resources

- *The Snow Queen* by Hans Christian Andersen
- DVD/CD musical version of *The Snow Queen*
- Instruments
- Plastic masks
- Card and paper
- Metallic collage materials
- Silver paint
- Scissors and glue

Cross-curricular Links

LITERACY: Write a review of the *Snow Queen* ballet. Explain that people (called critics) write in magazines and newspapers about productions, and people read them to help them decide if they want to see the show. Give examples of reviews and arrange for the children to watch a recording of the ballet.

Hiawatha

The 1855 epic poem *The Song of Hiawatha* by Henry Wadsworth Longfellow (1807–82) has long been a favourite classic. It has a rhythmic text with melodious Indian words and names. It is about Hiawatha's childhood, his journey into adulthood and then to the 'land of the hereafter.' As Hiawatha grows up, he learns the secrets of animals, magic and legends of his people. It is a romantic version of the story of a prophetic Indian leader who was responsible for creating the league of five nations in the sixteenth century.

Resources

- *The Song of Hiawatha* by Henry Wadsworth Longfellow
- Instruments
- Fabric collage materials
- Glue and scissors
- Large sheet of black fabric

Approach

1. Read the children the extract from *Hiawatha* about his childhood. Point out that it is a flowing rhythm consisting of a stressed syllable followed by an unstressed one. It is a monotonous rhythm and easy to imitate; encourage the children to lightly tap out the rhythm as it is read. Give the children copies of the text and read it together as a class, emphasising voices, pace, tone and expression. Develop the poem into a performance using drums beating in time as an accompaniment to their voices. Add more instruments as appropriate to portray different scenes.

2. Talk about the outdoor wilderness and images the poem evokes. Discuss how the poem stirs up the senses and reflects many aspects of nature. Allow the children to spend time studying the poem and choosing a particular part that inspires them.

3. Give the children a variety of fabric collage material (felt, hessian and so on) and ask them to visually interpret their chosen part of the poem.

4. Make large owls by cutting out triangles of felt to make the feathers and sticking them onto a hessian background.

5. Display the different scenes and the owls on a large piece of black fabric. Add stars to produce the night scene.

Cross-curricular Links

LITERACY: Make up another section to Hiawatha's poem. Look at the use of alliteration and repetition and encourage the children to incorporate the same techniques. Stress the importance of keeping the rhythm going. Try to include some speech between Hiawatha and Nokomis.

L'Enfant et les Sortilèges

Music and dance are intrinsically linked. Music makes people want to move, and dancing provides a way for people to join in musical entertainment. Dancing is a sociable activity and from disco to classical ballet, music contributes to the mood of the dance. *L'Enfant et les Sortilèges* (the child and the spells) is an opera written (from 1917 to 1925) by Maurice Ravel (1875–1937). It is set in an old fashioned Normandy country home and tells the story of a rude child who is reprimanded by the objects in his room which he has been destroying. The unhappy objects come to life, and the furniture and decorations begin to talk. In the second part, the bedroom becomes a garden full of things that have been tortured by the child. The opera concludes with the child learning his lesson, and understanding the consequences of his actions.

Resources

- *L'Enfant at les Sortilèges* by Maurice Ravel
- *Hockney Paints the Stage* by Martin Friedman (London Thames and Hudson)
- Cardboard boxes (shoe boxes)
- Collage materials
- Paint

Approach

1. Make the children familiar with the story and the various scenes within the opera. Explain that they are going to create a theatrical set for a backdrop to a scene from the opera. Show the children examples of David Hockney's set inspired by the opera by looking at *Hockney Paints the Stage* by Martin Friedman (London Thames and Hudson, 1983). Discuss his designs and link them to scenes within the story.

2. Give each child or group of children a scene from the opera: the dancing teapots, the torn figures from the decorative wallpaper, the bats in the garden, and ask them to design and make a stage set for this particular part of the opera.

3. Give each child a cardboard box to produce their ideas using a variety of collage material, including coloured card and sticky paper.

4. Display all the scenes together.

Degas' Little Dancer

Hilaire Germain Edgar Degas was born in Paris in 1834. He died in 1917 at the age of 83 and left behind 1200 paintings and sculptures, 300 of which depicted ballerinas. The origins of ballet go back 300 years earlier as a type of court entertainment. Louis XIV ruled France from 1643–1715 and founded the first ballet school.

Resources

- Ballet music
- *Degas and the Little Dancer* by Laurence Anholt (Barron's Education Series)
- Cartridge paper/sugar paper
- Pencils, chalk, charcoal, graphite
- Mod roc and bronze spray paint

Approach

1. Listen to excerpts of ballet music, such as *The Nutcracker*, *Swan Lake* or *Sleeping Beauty* by Peter Tchaikovsky or *Romeo and Juliet* by Sergei Prokofiev. In the first half of the nineteenth century, ballets had romantic themes whilst the second half of the century became the classical ballet period.

2. Tell the children the stories behind the most famous ballets, such as *Sleeping Beauty* by Tchaikovsky based on a fairy tale by the Frenchman, Charles Perrault.

3. Introduce the children to the artist Edgar Degas. Read the story of *Degas and the Little Dancer* by Laurence Anholt (Barron's Educational Series, 1996). Discuss how Degas would like to watch closely and make quick sketches to work on when he was back in the studio.

4. If possible, ask a child who is a budding ballerina to pose in a tutu for the class to sketch. Allow the model to choose various dancing positions for the class to make quick sketches/studies of, not forgetting to allow plenty of rest time for the model!

5. Allow children time to work on their drawings, then cut them out and display as one large dancing class composition.

6. Use mod roc to create a slightly 3-D version of *The Little Dancer*. Spray with bronze paint.

Flamenco Fan

All over the world people love to dance; consequently there are many different types of dance music. Dance music often has a strong beat to provide a framework for the movements. Flamenco is a rhythmic type of Spanish music and has evolved from the Gypsy and Arab music of Southern Spain. The guitar is very popular in Spain and is the main instrumental accompaniment to Flamenco singing and dancing.

Resources

- Flamenco music
- Pictures of Spanish fans/dancers
- Long strips of card
- Wax pastels
- Castanets

Approach

1. Play the children Spanish flamenco music, such as *Flamenco: Spanish Passion* by various artists (Brilliant Classics, 2005). Encourage them to close their eyes and let the music suggest patterns and colours. Ask the children how the music makes them feel and how it would make them want to move. If possible, show video clips of Spanish dancers with fans or show the children pictures of fans.

2. Ask the children to sketch out their ideas of patterns suggested by the music and talk about the colours best represented by the Spanish theme.

3. Give each child a long strip of card and ask them to transfer their ideas onto the card emphasising the need for abstract shapes and patterns rather than representational images.

Charles & Josette Lenars/CORBIS

4. Display all the individual strips together as a large Spanish fan.

5. Make individual smaller versions of flamenco fans and use them in a dance session where the children can move to the sounds of the Spanish guitar. Provide castanets to play as the children dance.

Cross-curricular Links

MODERN FOREIGN LANGUAGES: Look at the Spanish language and research words to display around the Spanish fan.

Blue Suede Shoes

Rock and Roll was created in the late 1940s. *Rock Around the Clock* by Bill Haley and His Comets (1954) is considered by many to be the song that put Rock and Roll on the international map. 'White' radio stations would previously not play 'black music' but Elvis Presley mixed rhythm and blues with country music and it was a huge commercial breakthrough. The stars of Rock and Roll were Elvis Presley, Bill Haley and His Comets, Buddy Holly and Jerry Lee Lewis. They were usually accompanied by two electric guitars, a bass guitar and drums. *Blue Suede Shoes,* written by Carl Perkins (1956) was one of Presley's biggest hits.

Resources

- Pictures of Rock and Roll fashion
- Rock and Roll music
- Pictures of album covers from the 1950s
- Templates of shoes cut from blue card
- Blue collage material
- Scissors and glue

LIBRARY, UNIVERSITY OF CHESTER

Approach

1. Rock and Roll music had a definitive style of fashion to accompany it. Men had long sideburns and hair greased into a quiff, tight black drainpipe trousers, and crepe-soled suede shoes or winkle pickers (black leather boots). Women would wear their hair tied back in a ponytail and wear flared knee length skirts and short socks. Show the children pictures of Rock and Roll fashion and play some famous Rock and Roll songs such as *Blue Suede Shoes* (1956) and *Rock Around the Clock* (1954).

2. Study a range of record/album covers of the time and ask the children to create a cover for *Blue Suede Shoes* using collage materials.

3. Give each child a template of a shoe cut from blue card and provide a variety of blue collage materials, including felt, string, art straws and blue paper. Demonstrate some ways the children could use these materials to make interesting patterns for their blue suede shoes.

4. Display in a circle like the shape of a record (examples may be needed to show the children what a single – 7" – record looked like!).

Fire

The four elements – earth, water, fire and wind – dominated natural philosophy for two hundred years and were developed by Greek philosophers. Although science has now discovered new ideas, the four main elements still illustrate the unity of life. Fire has the power to transform solids into liquids and gases. Its potential for destruction is awesome; the human need to harness it is great and not surprisingly it features strongly in the arts and music as it affects our emotions greatly.

Resources

- Pieces of fabric
- Elastic bands
- Yellow and red fabric dye
- Pictures of Tudor houses
- Cardboard
- Art straws
- Paint and brushes
- Iron

Approach

1. Teach the song *London's Burning* to the class. Discuss the historical background to the song (the Great Fire of London in 1666). *London Bridge is Falling Down* is also about this dramatic historical event. Divide the class into groups and explain how the song is going to be sung as a round. A round is a simple canon, where everyone sings the same tune but a few bars apart. Practice singing *London's Burning*, increasing the number of rounds as the children become more familiar with the tune and can concentrate on their part.

2. Give each child a piece of fabric. Fold the cloth forwards and backwards in a concertina fashion to create a striped effect. Tie with elastic bands. Stress the need to get the elastic bands as tight as possible.

3. When the fabric pieces are all tied, place them in a bucket of red or yellow dye for at least an hour. When dry, iron flat (only an adult should use the iron).

4. Display the squares as a patchwork of fire.

5. Study Tudor houses and use cardboard, paint, art straws and other materials to recreate them. Display in front of the 'fire'.

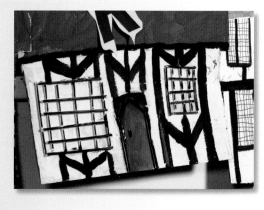

Cross-curricular Links

HISTORY: Study the period of history that surrounded the Great Fire of London. Research who the monarch was then and how people lived at this time.

Earth

Resources

- *Earth Song* by Michael Jackson
- Cartridge paper
- Large sheet of paper
- Pastels, glue and scissors
- Pictures from magazines and leaflets

Approach

1. Play a recording of *Earth Song* by Michael Jackson to the class. The lyrics are very moving and have a strong conservation and humanitarian theme. Discuss the lyrics and what mood they are conveying. Ask what the song is describing. What is Michael Jackson's message?

2. Introduce the idea of the world being like a huge jigsaw, with all of us inter-related and dependent upon each other. Ask the children to choose a part of the song that means something to them and sketch out some ideas to interpret it visually.

3. Divide a large sheet of paper into a jigsaw puzzle making sure each piece is numbered on the back to make it easy to reassemble.

4. Give each child a piece of the jigsaw and ask them to draw, colour and collage (using pictures from magazines and leaflets) their chosen part of the *Earth Song*.

5. Reassemble the pieces and display in the form of a large jigsaw.

Cross-curricular Links

ICT: Research one of the conservation issues featured in Michael Jackson's song, such as conservation of a particular animal. Ask the children to create a fact file about their issues and present it to the class.

Wind

Introducing children to the concept of wind as one of the four elements allows plenty of opportunity to study the family of wind instruments. Wind instruments work by making a column of air vibrate inside a tube and the more air there is vibrating, the lower the note sounds. Changing the length of the tube produces different notes. There are two types of wind instruments: woodwind and brass. The woodwind section includes flutes and piccolos, clarinets, oboes, bassoons and double bassoons and the brass section includes trombones, trumpets, tubas and French horns. They used to be made from wood or brass but now other materials may be used.

Approach

1. Introduce the class to as many woodwind instruments as possible and explain that the sound is made when you blow into a hollow object and the air starts to vibrate.

2. Experiment with making simple classroom wind instruments. For example, blow down a paper drinking straw, then cut the straw into different lengths to see if that alters the sound; blow across the top of bottles, then fill them with different amounts of water; make cardboard tubes into panpipes. Challenge the children to come up with as many different designs as possible and demonstrate their inventions to the rest of the class.

3. Some instruments have been designed to play 'nature's music' including the sound of the wind, for instance. Discuss aeolian harps and wind chimes. Ask the children to research these instruments and how they work.

4. Play the children a recording of *Let's Go Fly a Kite* from the film *Mary Poppins*. Talk about how the kite relies on air movement to stay in the sky. Write poems about kites soaring, twisting, playing and catching the wind. Children could read their poems to the class with background noise from the wind instruments.

5. To make kites, attach withies together with masking tape to make the frame. Mix PVA glue and water in a bowl and use a sponge to carefully cover a sheet of tissue paper with glue. Drape the tissue paper over the withie cane frame and cover with another layer of the PVA mixture so that the tissue dries hard. Embellish with collage material.

Resources

- Woodwind instruments
- Paper drinking straw
- Various bottles
- Cardboard tubes
- *Let's Go Fly a Kite* from *Mary Poppins*
- Withie canes and masking tape
- PVA glue and sponges
- Tissue paper
- Collage material

Cross-curricular Links

SCIENCE: Look at how we hear. Show a diagram of the human ear and explain how sound vibrations enable us to hear.

LITERACY: Read books that have wind themes, such as *The Wind in the Willows* by Kenneth Grahame. Compose poems about windy weather.

Water

Early music was probably inspired by the sound of wind, water, and birdsong. Musicians often use sounds made in the natural world within their compositions: Medwyn Goodall features the underwater songs of dolphins in *The Way of the Dolphin* and *Out of the Depths*. Terry Oldfield uses actual whale songs in his music. Much music has been composed reflecting the different forms of water – one of the most famous being George Frideric Handel's *Water Music*. Handel was born in Germany in 1685 but spent most of his adult life in England. Handel's *Water Music* suite was composed for King George I of England, and Handel and his orchestra followed the King's barge down the River Thames playing the music.

Resources for The Rainbow Display
- Water music
- Picture of *Raindrop* by Friedensreich Hundertwasser
- Cartridge paper and wax pastels

Approach

1. Allow the children to listen to a range of music on the theme of water: Handel's *Water Music*, *La Mer* by Claude Debussy, *Under the Sea* from Disney's *Little Mermaid* and the African-American spiritual *Wade in the Water*. In each case, discuss how the music reflects the nature of water. Ask them to try and identify the instruments they hear and what emotions they evoke.

2. Show the children copies of *Raindrop* by Friedensreich Hundertwasser (1928–2000); discuss the choice of colours and the displacement of shapes as if the raindrop has actually dropped into water.

3. Using a similar abstract technique, ask the children to design their own version of *Raindrop* using wax pastels on cartridge paper.

Approach

1. Teach the children the song *I Can Sing a Rainbow*. Although not strictly accurate with the rainbow spectrum (the true colours are red, orange, yellow, green, blue, indigo and violet) it provides a useful introduction to the science of the visible light spectrum.

2. Cut circles in different coloured card and give each child one. Provide a range of brightly-coloured material and ask the children to decorate their circle using only material in the card colour.

3. Display as a rainbow of coloured notes.

Resources for *I Can Sing a Rainbow* Display
- Card, glue and scissors
- Coloured card
- Collage material

Cross-curricular Links

SCIENCE: Look at how a rainbow is created when sunlight shines on falling rain and the light is split up by the raindrops into seven different colours which is seen as a rainbow. Make rainbow spinners out of card discs.

The Yellow Submarine

Resources

- The film *Yellow Submarine* (1968)
- Paint software (Dazzle Plus)
- Large sheet of card
- Paint and brushes

The film *Yellow Submarine* is an animated feature film based on music by The Beatles. The Beatles were at the peak of their popularity. The film is based on the age-old message that good can prevail over evil with the forces of love and good music. The story takes place in a paradise called 'Pepperland' where happiness reigned supreme, but was threatened by the terrible Blue Meanies who were determined to destroy all that was good. The title song of the film – *We all live in a yellow submarine* – provides the message that 'all our friends are aboard and there is no limit to the number of friends that can come aboard'.

Approach

1. Show the film *Yellow Submarine* or play The Beatles' song to the children. Explain to the children the concept behind the film. Use the Internet to find out more about the Beatles phenomenon and the songs within the film. Talk to the children about the art of animation.

2. Using paint software, such as Dazzle Plus, ask the children to create self portraits. Print out the pictures and cut each one out.

3. On a large sheet of card, draw a picture of the yellow submarine. Paint or cut out coloured pieces of card to create the different colours.

4. Display the class self portraits as a collage of faces all living in the yellow submarine.

Cross-curricular Links

ICT: Use animation software which allows the user to create a moving sequence of images as a short film that can be played back on the computer screen.

DESIGN TECHNOLOGY: Experiment with different ways of making moving pictures, for example a flip book.

Up, Up and Away

Approach

1. *Up, Up and Away* by Jimmy Webb is a song that uses the ideas of music and transport to sail away to a dream where the world is a nicer place. Study the lyrics of the song and invent sounds that may be appropriate to the words; for example, twinkling triangles may suggest stars.

2. This subject provides countless opportunities to develop the concept of where the children would fly to in their own beautiful balloon. Encourage the children to choose a particular country and research what they would see. Alternatively, they could think about flying to a completely imaginary place.

3. Listen to other music with a travelling theme: *Sailing* by Rod Stewart, *Trains, Boats and Planes* by Burt Bacharach, *Homeward Bound* by Simon and Garfunkel. Ask the children to imagine the destinations of the people travelling.

4. Blow up balloons (one per pair of children), papier mâché and allow to dry. Cut the balloons in half and give one half to each child.

5. Look at some pictures of decorated hot air balloons and give the children paper to design their own before painting their design onto the papier mâché.

6. Experiment with two-dimensional designs on paper and fabric.

7. Display the 2-D and 3-D balloons on a pale blue background alongside aerial photographs.

8. As an extension to this project, the children could draw aerial pictures showing the route their balloons took.

Resources

- *Up, Up and Away* by Jimmy Webb
- Balloons
- Papier mâché and glue
- Aerial view photographs
- Paint and brushes

Noah's Ark

Approach

1. Tell the Bible story of Noah's Ark (Genesis, chapters 6–9).

2. Introduce the song and lyrics for *The Animals Went in Two by Two.* Show the children the book by Jan Pienkowski (Walker books, 2003). Encourage the class to get to know the song by singing a short section with the children echoing. Each verse has the same four-line format; show the children a copy of the song and ask them to pick out similarities, differences and rhyming patterns in each verse.

3. Each of the six verses end with the line 'and they all went into the ark, for to get out of the rain'. Discuss ways of making the sound of the rain to accompany this part of the song (tapping fingers on tables, using shakers and so on).

4. Give each child two sheets of card and ask them to choose an animal – not necessarily one that features in the song. Ask the children to make two identical pictures of their chosen animal and cut them out. Decorate with coloured card or sticky paper.

5. Make a large card picture of the ark.

6. Stick each pair of animals onto the ark giving them a 3-D effect by placing small pieces of card between the two animals.

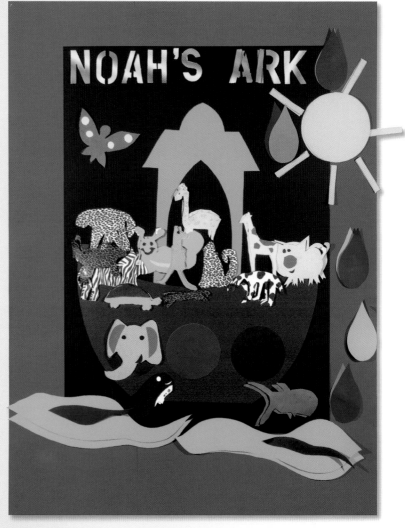

Resources

- The Bible
- *The Animals Went in Two by Two* by Jan Pienkowski
- Card
- Coloured card and sticky paper
- Glue and scissors

Cross-curricular Links

DRAMA: Ask the children to work in pairs or small groups and choose an animal to pretend to be. Ask the children to consider how their animal would move and sound. Develop a sequence of movements to get into the ark. Encourage them to move identically as a group, and ask the rest of the class to guess which animal they have chosen to portray.

Wheels on the Bus

Resources

- Card and string
- Scissors and glue
- Cartridge paper
- Paint and brushes
- Variety of instruments

Approach

1. *The Wheels on the Bus* is an action song which young children always enjoy singing. Introduce the song to the children, make up actions for each verse and add sounds. The sounds can be made using a variety of classroom instruments or voice sounds.

2. Think about other vehicles with wheels and change the title of the song. Ask the children for ideas about the sounds that a different vehicle would make in its daily life, for example, 'The wheels on the tractor go splush, splush, splush'. Make up sounds to accompany the new song.

3. Give the children a piece of card, string and glue. Prepare a 'string print' by drawing a circle and sticking string around the outline. Add wheel spokes. Allow to dry.

4. Paint the raised string area in a chosen colour and press down firmly. Develop into a pattern.

Cross-curricular Links

MATHS: Carry out a traffic survey and monitor all the different vehicles that pass by the school in a half-hour period. Draw graphs to illustrate the ratio of different vehicles.

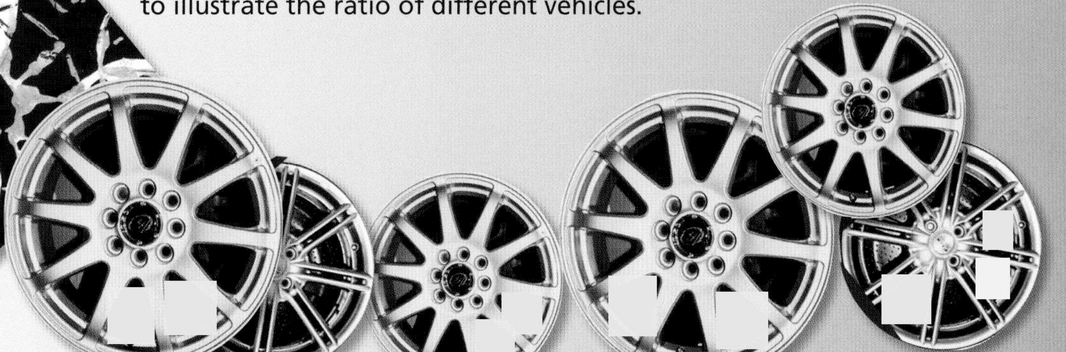

Paul Klee Display

Paul Klee (1879–1940) is one of the most admired artists of the last century and was a man of many talents. He excelled not only as an artist, but also as a musician, poet, teacher and philosopher. He was born into a family of musicians and he himself was an accomplished violinist. His love of music was a powerful force behind his visual creations. One of his friends once remarked that 'Klee the painter is unthinkable without Klee the musician'. Paul Klee's artistic work reflects his relationship with music and many of his paintings have titles that refer directly to music.

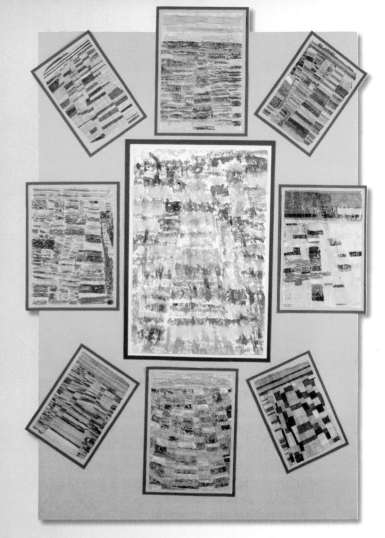

Resources

- Various pictures by Paul Klee
- Various pictures by Wassily Kandinsky
- Papyrus sheets and yellow ink
- Felt pens
- Paper and wax crayons/pastels

Approach

1. Show the children pictures of Klee's artwork and ask them what they can 'see' and 'hear'. Encourage them to think what type of music it reminds them of. Paul Klee's work was inspired by a passion for music, but it is difficult to find reference to the type of music he enjoyed. Show the children examples such as *Moonrise – Sunset* (1940) and ask the children to think about the music that may have inspired him.

2. Look at Klee's work *Highway and Byways* (1929). It is perhaps one of his most famous paintings and was inspired by a visit to Egypt to celebrate his 50th birthday. The composition owes a lot to the Egyptian terrain and in it he suggests roads travelling from fertile plains to the Nile with the blue of the sky at the top of the picture. Klee painted on many different textures to suit his subject matter, including newspapers, cloth, cardboard, many types of paper, glass and metal.

3. To create a paper batik version of *Highway and Byways* use wax crayons or pastels. To produce the scene, roughly crease the paper, unfold and cover with a layer of yellow ink. If using papyrus, felt pens are easiest for children to manage.

4. Encourage the children to experiment with other surfaces, as Klee did, and ask them to suggest music to go with their pictures.

5. Explore also Wassily Kandinsky's (1866–1944) relationship with music and art, and how he tried to reflect the sounds of instruments in his colourful paintings.

Cross-curricular Links

HISTORY: Study the terrain of Ancient Egypt and look at some of the pyramids and temples Klee may have visited in 1928 which inspired the composition of *Highway and Byways*.

Matisse Display

Explain that jazz was developed around 1900 in New Orleans from black, American music like blues and ragtime. In the 1940s some jazz musicians invented modern jazz, called 'Bebop'. There are many different forms of jazz and the first jazz musicians usually played spontaneously, by ear, in bands with trumpets, trombones and clarinets.

Resources

- Jazz music
- Pictures of Henri Matisse's *Jazz* collection
- Brightly-coloured paper
- Cartridge paper
- Glue and scissors

Approach

1. Play the children some jazz music: *Dixieland Jazz* (Avid, 2006) and *Hot Fives and Sevens* box set by Louis Armstrong (JSP, 1999), and *The Best of Glenn Miller* by Glenn Miller (St Clair).

2. Show the class some of Henri Matisse's (1869–1954) jazz-inspired pictures. Explain a little about his life and that in his later years, when illness prevented him from painting, Matisse cut out shapes from brightly-coloured paper then arranged them on a background. He then had assistants take these collages to be printed. *Jazz* is considered one of his most ambitious and important series of work. Matisse often turned to music and dance for inspiration and jazz evoked for Matisse the idea of movement and rhythm. Many felt that Matisse had taught the eye to 'hear' with jazz cut-outs, and this style of cut-out became his trademark.

3. Allow the children to experiment with bold, clashing colours using brightly-coloured pieces of paper and create a jazz cut-out in the style of Matisse's work. Emphasise to the children that the shapes should portray movement and rhythm.

Fingal's Cave

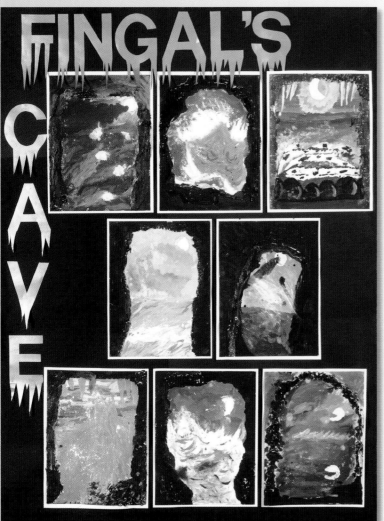

The Hebrides Overture, also known as Fingal's Cave, was written in the 1830s by Felix Mendelssohn (1809–1847); a pianist, organist and conductor who began composing in his early teens. In the nineteenth century it was fashionable for wealthy young men to embark on a tour of Europe to further their education and gain perspective and culture. Mendelssohn undertook one such tour and visited the renowned Fingal's Cave in Scotland. The beauty and magnitude of the place had a tremendous effect upon him and he quickly wrote down the opening notes to the overture, which was finished over a year later. About this time, composers were beginning to use music to express their feelings and emotions and even to tell stories. Mendelssohn's overture depicts the physical world of the cave in striking terms – the listeners are invited to hear the breaking of the waves, see the basalt columns and geographic wonders, and marvel at the overwhelming vastness of the cavern.

Resources

- *The Hebrides Overture* by Felix Mendelssohn
- Pictures of Fingal's Cave
- Cartridge paper
- Paint and brushes

Approach

1. Introduce the term 'romantic music', which describes music predominantly composed in the nineteenth century that was inspired by nature and other arts, such as poetry and painting. Composers, as well as painters and writers, tried to use their art to express emotions and personal feelings. Musicians invented all kinds of interesting and clever ways to show non-musical concepts in sound. This movement lasted until the early 1900s.

2. Listen to excerpts of *The Hebrides Overture* by Felix Mendelssohn and look at the pictures of Fingal's Cave at the same time. Encourage the children to listen for the breaking waves and talk about how Mendelssohn has created the vastness and awesome splendour of the cavern.

3. Using both the music and photographs of the cave for inspiration, ask the children to recreate the scene with paint. Encourage them to experiment with the great movement of waves and different colours for the sky to create atmosphere.

Cross-curricular Links

SCIENCE: Study the invention of photography in 1838. Discuss what early photographs of the cave would have looked like and how photography has developed over the years.

Sea Shell Patterns

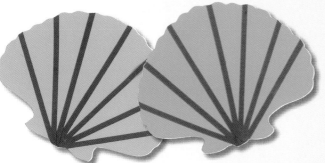

Resources

- *Cockles and Mussels* song
- Shells
- Coloured wax pastels

Approach

1. Play the song *Cockles and Mussels* (also known as *Molly Malone*) to the class. (Song and lyrics are available on the Internet.) The song is well-known and easy to sing for young children. The mood of the song is upbeat even though poor Molly Malone dies from a fever and becomes a ghost! If the children are old enough, put the song in historical context from centuries past, explaining some of the unfamiliar language.

2. Divide the children into groups and encourage each group to sing one of the verses with everyone joining in with the chorus.

3. Using a shell or a shell template demonstrate how to draw round it to create interesting shapes and patterns.

4. Allow the children to experiment with designs before choosing their favourite. Fill in designs using brightly-coloured wax pastels.

Underwater Display

Approach

1. Making music involves singing, dancing, moving, composing, listening and many more inter-related activities, which help children engage with the sounds they hear. Play the children a selection of water/sea music (Enya's *Watermark* [Warner, 1998] or Claude Debussy's piano piece *Poissons d'Or* from *Images II*) and ask them to imagine the marine life within the ocean waves. Discuss the creatures, their movements and habitats. In PE encourage the children to move around in a way that expresses their response to the water and the sea life within it. Use the classroom instruments to accompany their movements.

2. Give each child a sheet of cartridge paper and ask them to draw and colour an exotic tropical fish using wax pastels.

3. Fill a tray with water and demonstrate the process of creating swirling seawater by dropping marbling ink into the water and moving it in circular movements. Place a sheet of cartridge paper on top of the water to 'print' the marbling pattern. Allow to dry.

4. Cut out the coloured fish and stick onto the marbling background.

5. To make the silk fish, draw an outline in the silk gutta and allow each child to paint one of the scales in brightly-coloured silk paints. The resulting class composition will be vibrant and varied as each child brings a different pattern to the design.

6. Display with paper seaweed on a blue background.

Resources

- Music with sea/water/fish themes
- Instruments
- Wax pastels
- Cartridge paper
- Marbling inks
- Water tray
- Large piece of silk
- Silk paints
- Silk gutta
- Scissors and glue

Frank Meadow Sutcliffe

Shanties are sea songs which were sung by working sailors during the time of the great sailing ships. The golden age of the shanties was the mid-nineteenth century. Shanties provided a way for sailors to express themselves without fear of punishment; they helped to keep their spirits up and to work together. There are different types of shanties: the three main ones being short haul ones for tasks requiring quick pulls over a short period of time, such as raising the mast head; halyard shanties which were sung during the raising and lowering of sails; and capstan shanties for very long repetitive tasks, such as winding up the heavy anchor chain.

Resources

- Sea shanties
- Pictures of Whitby by Frank Meadow Sutcliffe
- Cartridge paper
- Tea bags
- Sepia coloured ink
- Ink pens
- Photographic paper
- Developer
- Fixer and tongs
- Three trays
- Paintbrushes

Approach

1. Play the children some sea shanties, such as *The Drunken Sailor*. Share the background to sea shanties and ask them how they would feel about the songs if they were sailors. Explain how the sailors would have often adapted the lyrics to a song depending on the task that had to be done. Discuss the jobs that would be required on board a nineteenth-century sailing ship and ask the children to compose an alternative song that the sailors might have sung. Set the words to the tune of *The Drunken Sailor.*

2. Show the children pictures of Whitby taken by the photographer Frank Meadow Sutcliffe around the time of the sea shanties. Discuss the sepia colour and demonstrate how this can be recreated on a sheet of cartridge paper stained by soaking a tea bag in warm water, and then wiping it over the paper.

3. Using ink pens and sepia ink, the children could copy detailed ships onto the stained paper.

4. Tell the class they are to create photographic 'reproductions' of Sutcliffe's work. Fill one plastic tray with water. Following the instructions on the bottles, mix the developer with water in the second tray, and mix the fixer with water in the third tray. It is important to caution them about using chemicals. Although perfectly safe if handled correctly, chemicals must not go near the eyes or mouth.

5. Remove a sheet of photographic paper from its black bag and paint on waves for the sea using a paintbrush dipped in developer.

6. Using tongs, submerge the paper into the fixer for about five minutes. Then, soak the paper in the final tray of water for at least ten minutes. Dry flat.

7. Finally, children can use pen and ink to add a nineteenth-century sailing ship.

Cross-curricular Links

HISTORY: Captain James Cook (1728–79) had his crews sign articles for his sea voyages to the pacific in Whitby. Chart his explorations.

LITERACY: Read *The Herring Girls* by Theresa Tomlinson (Corgi Childrens, 2005). It is a historical novel set in Whitby using Sutcliffe's photographs as stimuli. Write personal stories based on different photographs.

Seascapes

Resources

- Recording of *Skye Boat Song* and lyrics
- Photographs of Scottish landscapes
- Map showing Skye
- Cartridge paper
- Paint and brushes

Approach

1. Play the class the *Skye Boat Song* and discuss its historical background. In 1746, Prince Charlie's rebel army was defeated by the Duke of Cumberland at the Battle of Culloden. Prince Charlie went into hiding and fled to Skye helped by Flora Macdonald. As a class, discuss other historical based songs and their social context, such as *Ring a Ring a Roses*, which is about the plague.

2. Sing the *Skye Boat Song,* giving each group a particular verse to work on.

3. Show the children photographs of the Scottish landscape. Talk about the colours, the movement of the waves, and how the landscape would change at different times of the day and throughout the year.

4. Locate Skye on a map and discuss the type of journey Prince Charlie would have had from mainland Scotland to Skye.

5. Glue the photographs onto a large sheet of cartridge paper and challenge the children to mix colours as accurately as possible to match the photograph and make the scene fill the paper.

Cross-curricular Links

ICT: Encourage the children to access the Internet to find out about Prince Charlie and other songs with a historical context.

Indian Musical Sticks

Music is a way of celebrating and communicating feelings in all cultures. People in different parts of the world have their own particular instruments and styles of music and singing. Many festivals in India are celebrated with the sounds of stringed instruments called 'sitars', which is probably the best known of all Indian instruments and is played by plucking the strings – seven on the outside and between nine and thirteen on the inside. The sound of the sitar can be heard in the accompaniment to the song *Norwegian Wood* by The Beatles. Rhythm sticks are used to accompany flourishes of dancing in India often associated with joyous religious festivals, for example Holi.

Approach

1. Listen to examples of Indian music, such as *Il Stad Imrat Khan* and *Classical Indian Sitar & Surbahar Ragas* by Sarwar Sabri and Baluji Shrivastav. Explain that although some examples may seem as if they have no apparent structure, each type of music has its own particular pattern and characteristic structure. Indian music is traditionally not written down and instead musicians learn patterns of notes called 'ragas' and rhythms called 'talas'. There are hundreds of 'ragas', each designed for a different season or time of day. Include a range of listening material from Bollywood dancing to traditional raga melodies. Children could also listen to *Norwegian Wood* by The Beatles (from the album *Rubber Soul*, 1965).

2. Paint cardboard tubes black and allow to dry.

3. Using matchsticks dipped in paint, children can create brightly-coloured patterns on top of the black paint. Encourage the children to return their matchstick to the paint pot every three or four dots to get the brightest patterns.

4. Embellish with strips of felt or coloured paper and attach the bells.

Resources

- Indian music
- Cardboard tubes
- Paint and brushes
- Matchsticks
- Bells
- Strips of felt and coloured paper

Cross-curricular Links

PE: Learn Bollywood dances.

RE: Find out more about Indian festivals, such as Holi.

African Fabric and Drums

African music is often fast and rhythmic, and includes many instruments – most prominently, dozens of different shapes and sizes of drums. African music is full of complicated ever-changing patterns. Singing, dancing and playing instruments are an important part of everyday life. Different parts of Africa are associated with different types of drums, which can be made from wood, clay or dried gourds (a vegetable shell). The one thing they all have in common is a hollow base with a skin stretched tightly over the top which vibrates when hit, making the air inside the base vibrate too.

Resources

- African music
- African fabrics
- Various drums
- Pieces of cloth
- Paintbrushes
- Clay plant pots
- Chamois leather
- String

Approach

1. Introduce the idea of African music to the children and explain that Africa is a huge continent with many different styles of music. Play tracks from *The Best of Ladysmith Black Mambazo* (Shanachie, 1992) and encourage the children to identify the instruments and rhythms.

2. Give the children a selection of drums. Demonstrate a rhythm which accentuates the first of every four beats: 1234, 1234, 1234; do the same with a three-beat rhythm. Divide the class into groups and ask different groups to beat different rhythms simultaneously.

3. Look at examples of African cloth designs; discuss the patterns and vibrant colours.

4. Ask the children to use a pencil to sketch onto cloth a design based on some of the patterns and images they have noted from the examples. Designs should then be painted in chosen colours.

5. To make drums, ask the children to paint designs onto plant pots. When dry, place the pots bottom to bottom and stretch a round piece of chamois leather over both ends. Attach firmly by threading strings from the top of the drum to the bottom.

6. Use the drums to accompany some rhythmic African music.

Cross-curricular Links

GEOGRAPHY: Look at the many different countries that make up the continent of Africa. Give each group a country to research and report back to the class.

Japanese Gongs and Origami

Music and dancing has always been important in far Eastern countries. In Japan, there is a form of musical play which takes place on an empty stage called 'Noh', which combines music, poetry, dance and costume. Traditional instruments to accompany the dancing would be drums, flutes and a stringed instrument called a 'shamisen' used in Kabuki drama. Gongs are also popular in China and Japan. In many far Eastern countries, owning a gong was a sign of wealth. Gongs can be made in different thicknesses, playing different pitches, and can be very elaborate.

Resources

- Japanese music
- Pictures of elaborate gongs
- Large circular pieces of card
- Pasta shapes and string
- Glue
- Gold/silver spray
- Origami paper and designs

Approach

1. Discuss Japanese music and play some tracks from *Koto Music of Japan* by various artists. Look at examples of far Eastern gongs. Explain that most gongs have a 'playing spot' where the sound is the fullest, and as part of an orchestra the boom of a gong can be powerful in bringing a piece of music to a conclusion. If possible, try to play some music which concludes in this way and discuss its impact.

2. Gongs are made from metal and therefore difficult to recreate with children, but the patterns of embellishments can be studied and made using string and pasta shapes. Each child should draw a pattern on a large circular sheet of card, apply plenty of glue and place pasta shapes or string to make the design.

3. Once dry, the designs can be sprayed silver or gold.

4. Introduce the children to the art of origami (paper folding). There are plenty of simple origami designs available; choose one, such as a flower. Demonstrate how to create the folds and allow the children to experiment with this traditional Japanese craft.

5. Display individual contributions as a class creation.

Cross-curricular Links

LITERACY: Study the poetic form of Haiku. Copy out Haiku poems onto origami paper structures.

The Nutcracker

Pyotr (Peter) Ilyich Tchaikovsky was born in Russia in 1840. *The Nutcracker* ballet, choreographed by Lev Ivanov, was first performed in 1892. The story is based on a German tale by ETA Hoffmann. It takes place on Christmas Eve and two children, Clara and Fritz, are having a party. Clara's favourite gift is a nutcracker in the shape of a doll, which comes to life during the night. Clara goes downstairs to see the Nutcracker dancing with the other toys, when suddenly an army of mice appear led by the fierce Mouse King. A battle ensues, and just when it appears the Mouse King will win, Clara throws her slipper at him. The Nutcracker is saved and is transformed into a handsome fairy prince, who takes Clara into a fantastic kingdom of sweets. Here, Clara meets the Sugar Plum Fairy who offers them delicious cakes and sweets, and summons a series of entertainers, including Spanish and Russian dancers. There are several different endings to this story; sometimes the ballet ends with Clara and her prince setting off together to explore the future, or more commonly with Clara under the Christmas tree fast asleep having had a magical dream.

Tchaikovsky composed *The Nutcracker Suite* (a collection of short instrumental pieces forming a complete work) in 1891–2.

Approach

1. Play the children part of *The Nutcracker*, for example, the dance of the Sugar Plum Fairy. Tell the story of *The Nutcracker* to put the piece of music in context.

2. Explain to the children that Tchaikovsky aimed to create different sounds for all the dances and followed the choreographer's instructions closely. Ask the children to imagine what sort of dance the Sugar Plum Fairy would be performing to the music and, if possible, allow them the time and space to develop their own movements (perhaps in PE). Contrast the Sugar Plum Fairy's dance with the Russian dance.

3. Ask the children to consider what sort of stage design would be appropriate to complement the dances in the land of sweets. Encourage the children to be inspired by the colours and textures of sweets and candy. Give the children a selection of cardboard tubes, lolly sticks and collage materials including tissue, crêpe and sticky paper. Ask them to create a stage backdrop for the land of sweets.

Cross-curricular Links

LITERACY: Explore different endings to the ballet, and ask the children to write their own version avoiding the option of 'it was just a dream'.

Resources

- *The Nutcracker* by Tchaikovsky
- Cardboard tubes
- Lolly sticks
- Paper collage materials
- Glue and scissors

Ten Green Bottles

Resources

- Variety of green bottles
- Green card
- Collage material
- Paint and brushes
- Scissors and glue

Approach

1. Look at the collection of green bottles; discuss their shape, patterns, what they are made from and what they contained. Demonstrate how bottles can be used to make simple instruments by pouring water into them and blowing across the top. Point out how the note gets lower as you add more water. The pitch of the note varies because of the different lengths of the air columns in the bottles. Try tapping the bottles; experimenting with the pitch. Does the fullest bottle give the lowest note when tapped? Challenge the children to arrange several bottles filled with different amounts of water in order of pitch.

2. Introduce the song *Ten Green Bottles*. Ask the children to invent some sounds to accompany it using the musical bottles.

3. The class could decorate green card bottles using collage material. Encourage the children to work in groups and experiment with a different art technique for each bottle, for example quilling (rolling up strips of paper), fabric painting and pastel patterns.

4. Sing other counting songs, such as *This Old Man*.

Cross-curricular Links

LITERACY: Explore the colour green – songs, rhymes, sayings associated with the colour, such as *The Green-Eyed Monster*, 'Greenpeace', 'green fingers', 'green light' or 'grass is always greener'. Make up poems about the colour green.

Oranges and Lemons

Approach

1. Introduce the children to the nursery rhyme *Oranges and Lemons*. Talk to the children about the words and explain any new ones, such as 'farthings'. The song is sung during a playground game; explain the game and let the children play it.

2. Give the children photographs of different types of fruit and vegetables. Stick the photographs onto a larger sheet of cartridge paper. Look at the colour and texture of the fruit; demonstrate ways of mixing paint to match the different shades.

3. Ask the children to continue each photograph using carefully mixed colours to create more of the same fruit or vegetable.

4. Display as a large 'fruit and veg' stall with a canopy made out of red and white card.

Resources
- Cartridge paper
- Photographs of fruit and vegetables
- Paint
- Brushes
- Red and white card

Cross-curricular Links

DESIGN AND TECHNOLOGY: Look at recipes that use oranges and lemons to make drinks. Children could invent their own recipe, write a list of ingredients and the method. They could design the bottle packaging for their drink.

GEOGRAPHY: Look at the countries where oranges and lemons come from. Discuss what growing conditions they need.

PSHCE: Look at the role fruit and vegetables play in a healthy diet. List fruits and arrange a tasting session.

MATHS: Chart favourite fruits and make graphs.

Oats and Beans and Barley Grow

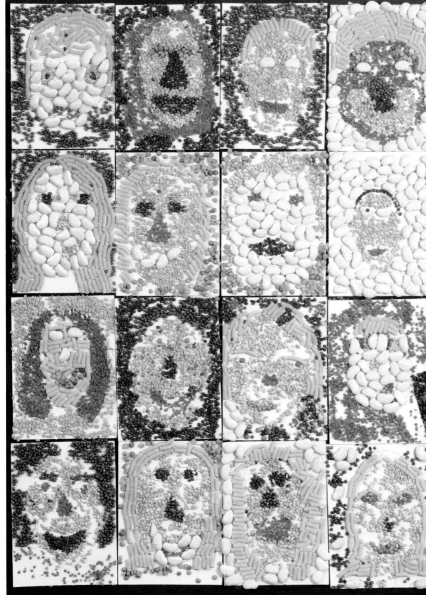

Approach

1. Teach the children the song *Oats and Beans and Barley Grow*. Encourage the children to tap the beat in the different lines.

2. Make shakers to accompany the song by giving the children a collection of plastic bottles, tins and boxes with tops and lids. Fill them with the oats and beans. Try varying the amounts and compare the different sounds they make.

3. Give each child a piece of card and several different types of pulses (preferably out-of-date produce). Ask the children to draw a sketch of themselves, and use the different coloured pulses to build up the picture.

4. Display the portraits together.

Resources

- Plastic bottles, tins and boxes
- Pieces of card
- Dried oats, beans, barley
- Glue and scissors

Lion King Display

Musicals are plays that not only have singing but also include acting and dancing. They developed from light opera, but unlike opera the characters often speak a lot as well as sing. The musical *The Lion King* is based on a Disney film; the music is by Elton John and the lyrics by Tim Rice. It tells the story of Simba, prince of the African lions, who fights with his evil uncle Scar for the throne after his uncle kills his father, Mufasa, and blames Simba for the murder.

Approach

1. Listen to music from the CD *The Lion King* (Walt Disney, 2006) and talk about the story behind the musical and how Simba eventually takes his rightful place in the 'circle of life'. Explain how musicals often tell a story using a mixture of singing, acting and dancing and ask the children if they can name any others.

2. Look at the Disney images from *The Lion King*. Talk about the possible differences between the stage musical and the Disney film.

3. Give the children cartridge paper and demonstrate ways of colouring the background by using sponges dipped in various shades of yellow and orange.

4. Allow the children the opportunity to sketch out some simple images of a lion, and when they are happy with their design, paint it onto their coloured cartridge paper with black paint.

5. Display around a large lion's head made out of crêpe, tissue and curled cartridge paper. Include palm trees for effect.

Resources

- *The Lion King* CD
- Pictures from *The Lion King*
- Cartridge paper
- Yellow, orange and black paint
- Brushes, scissors and glue
- Sponges
- Tissue, crêpe and cartridge paper

Cats Display

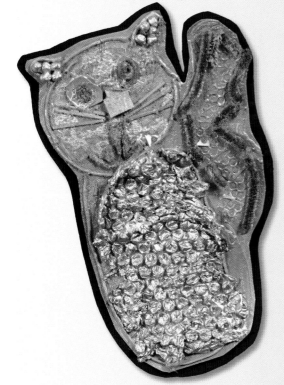

Resources

- *Cats* CD
- Poems by TS Elliot
- Paper
- Collage materials
- Silver spray

Approach

1. The musical *Cats*, written by Andrew Lloyd Webber, is based on TS Elliot's poems. Play music from the *Cats* CD (Polydor, 2005)and read some of the poems. Explain that *Cats* is one of the longest running musicals in the history of the theatre. Talk about the link between the poems and the musical and how dance is a very prominent feature of this particular musical.

2. Discuss the characteristics of cats and encourage children to sketch out ideas on a piece of paper.

3. The children could then develop their sketches into 3-D pictures of cats, using a variety of collage materials (including dried pasta and string).

4. When dry, spray silver and display on a black background.

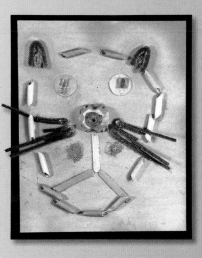

Cross-curricular Links

LITERACY: Read TS Elliot's poems on cats and write own poems about a lion.

PE: Develop a 'cats' dance sequence – creeping, freezing, leaping, pouncing, stretching and curling.

Joseph and the Amazing Technicolour Dreamcoat

Resources

- *Joseph and the Amazing Technicolour Dreamcoat* CD
- Bible story of Joseph
- Pieces of cloth
- Brightly-coloured paint
- Brushes

Approach

1. *Joseph and the Amazing Technicolour Dreamcoat* was Andrew Lloyd Webber's first big hit; the song lyrics are by Tim Rice. It was written as a school rock musical. Explain how the musical is based on the Bible story of Joseph; read the story and play songs from the musical.

2. Talk about how there is no talking in this musical and the whole story is told through song. Discuss the title of the musical and why it was chosen.

3. Give each child a piece of cloth cut out in the shape of a coat. Ask them to design a new coat for Joseph using many different colours.

4. Provide a variety of brightly-coloured paints for the children to use.

5. Display alongside a larger version of a new coat for Joseph.

Cross-curricular Links

PSHCE: Explore the emotions of the characters involved in the Joseph story, from jealousy to fear and joy at being reunited. Re-write the tale from the perspective of one of the characters in the story, including references to the differing emotions experienced.

Magic Flute Display

An opera is a play set to music. Opera as we know it today was created in Florence, in Italy, at the beginning of the seventeenth century. Opera singers must be able to act as well as sing, as they have to use their voices and faces to express the feelings of the characters as very often the operas are performed with scripts in their original languages. People argue that it does not particularly matter if the audience do not understand the words, as the music has a language of its own.

Resources

- *The Magic Flute* by Wolfgang Amadeus Mozart
- Story of *The Magic Flute*
- Flute
- Wax pastels
- Cartridge paper
- Marbling inks
- Water tray
- Feathers
- Stars/sequins

Approach

1. Read the story *The Magic Flute* by Anne Gatti (Chronicle Books, 2005) and then play the music by Wolfgang Amadeus Mozart (1756–91). Encourage the children to match up the story with the exerpts from the music. Show the children a flute and demonstrate the sounds it makes.

2. Identify the main characters of the story and discuss the part they play.

3. Study the characters of the Queen of the Night (sometimes known as the Starry Queen) and Papageno (the bird catcher). Explore how they could be portrayed visually.

4. Ask the children to choose a character to draw, and give each child a piece of cartridge paper and wax pastels to draw their character. Cut out when finished.

5. Demonstrate the process of creating marbling backgrounds by dropping marbling ink into the water. Try combing it in circular movements, and then placing a piece of cartridge paper onto the ink to soak up the pattern.

6. Invite each child to choose an appropriately coloured background. When dry, stick their cut-out character onto the piece of paper.

7. Embellish with stars (for the Queen of the Night) or feathers (for Papageno).

71

Madame Butterfly

Resources

- Music from *Madame Butterfly*
- Withie canes
- Masking tape
- Tissue paper
- PVA glue
- Sponges
- Tissue paper

Approach

1. Explain that Giacomo Puccini (1858–1924), one of Italy's greatest opera composers, wrote *Madame Butterfly* in 1904 at a time when there was great interest in Japanese culture. Talk about the different types of voices opera singers have: soprano (name of the highest female voice); tenor (name of a male voice with a medium to high range); baritone (male voice that is medium, between bass and tenor); bass (deepest male voice). Explain how some of these terms can apply to instruments. Play some of the music from *Madame Butterfly* and try to identify some of these different voices.

2. Soak the withie canes in water for an hour or so to make them more pliable. Demonstrate how to bend the canes into butterfly shapes and secure with masking tape.

3. Make a mix of PVA glue and water in a bowl and use a sponge to carefully cover a sheet of tissue paper with the mixture.

4. Drape the tissue over the butterfly frame and cover with another layer of PVA glue so that the tissue dries hard.

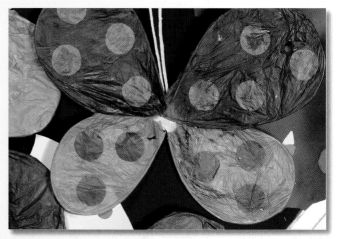

Cross-curricular Links

SCIENCE: Study how we produce sound from the air in our lungs vibrating the vocal cords. Discover why men's voices are deeper than women's.

LIBRARY, UNIVERSITY OF CHESTER